THE ULTIMATE UK AIR FRYER COOKBOOK FOR BEGINNERS

800 Days Easy and Affordable Frying Recipes with Colour Pictures | Compatible for Any Air Fryer Model to Enjoy Everyday

Roger N Trent

Copyright © 2023 By Roger N Trent All rights reserved.

No part of this book may be reproduced, transmitted, or distributed in any form or by any means without permission in writing from the publisher except in the case of brief quotations embodied in critical articles or reviews.

Legal & Disclaimer

The content and information in this book is consistent and truthful, and it has been provided for informational, educational and business purposes only.

The illustrations in the book are from the website shutterstock.com, depositphoto.com and freepik.com and have been authorized.

The content and information contained in this book has been compiled from reliable sources, which are accurate based on the knowledge, belief, expertise and information of the Author. The author cannot be held liable for any omissions and/or errors.

Table of Contents

1   **INTRODUCTION**

2   **CHAPTER 1**

THE AIR FRYER 101

6   **CHAPTER 2**

BREAKFASTS

12   **CHAPTER 3**

VEGETABLES

19   **CHAPTER 4**

POULTRY

29   **CHAPTER 5**

FISH AND SEAFOOD

38   **CHAPTER 6**

MEATS

46 CHAPTER 7

WRAPS AND SANDWICHES

50 CHAPTER 8

SNACKS AND DESSERTS

58 CHAPTER 9

FAST AND EASY EVERYDAY FAVOURITES

64 APPENDIX 1

AIR FRYER TIME TABLE

APPENDIX 2

68 **RECIPES INDEX**

INTRODUCTION

Having delicious food every day and staying in shape is now made possible, all thanks to the fast, efficient and oil-free cooking technology of air fryers. Now that I have spent six years of my life cooking with air fryers, I can't help but wonder what my life would have been without them! Air fryers make everyday cooking so simple and effortless that I don't mind cooking at home even after a lengthy day at work; I try all my favourite recipes without the fear of extra calories. Air frying has allowed me to keep my weight controlled while enjoying all the crispy snacks, entrees, and desserts. So the claims of air fryers being a healthy alternative to deep oil frying or other frying methods are one hundred per cent true, and I couldn't agree more. My air-frying experience has been great so far, and I want you to have the same! So with this cookbook comes a complete range of delicious and easy-to-cook air fryer recipes that you can try to meet all your nutritional needs while staying healthy.

CHAPTER 1
The Air Fryer 101

Air-Fryer: A Must-To-Have for Every Kitchen ·· 3

How to Set it Up ········· 3

How to Air Fry ········· 3

Getting the Best Out of Air Fryer ········· 4

After-Cook Cleaning ········· 5

It is true that air fryers come in various different sizes and models, and each version comes with its own specific features, but the basic working of every air fryer is the same, so as long as you follow the following the simple steps, you can cook the best of the meals in your air fryer.

Air-Fryer: A Must-To-Have for Every Kitchen

Air fryers have practically made oil-free frying possible. The crispy texture of the oil-fried product can now be achieved through the hot air convection inside the cooking chamber of the air fryers. Inside an air fryer, there is a heating element and a fan that throws hot air at such a pressure that it hits the food particles and turns them crispy from the outside. The overall high heat inside the cooking chamber meanwhile cooks the food from the inside. By doing so, an air fryer offers several amazing benefits.

- **Healthier Cooking**

The benefit of healthier cooking is the single most significant factor for the majority of individuals purchasing an air fryer. This is the ideal technique to make unhealthy deep-fried items with healthier ones because it uses very little oil in the cooking process.

- **Safe and Easy to Use**

We all would like to cook more frequently at home these days, but we just don't have the time to do it. Because of this, even though we are aware of how unhealthy quick meals and takeout are, they are still very popular. Would you rather order takeout if you could cook things like salmon or pork chops in the air fryer in less than 20 minutes? Cooking at home with convenience is a far more appealing option due to air fryers' speed and ease of usage. Preparing dinner is made easier by the air fryer. Even if it's frozen, simply season a piece of meat, like a chicken breast, put it in the basket, and set the timer for cooking and voila! The meal will be ready in just a few minutes.

- **Crisp and Crunchy Food**

You'll enjoy this reason the most if you frequently prepare frozen and breaded meals like chicken tenders, nuggets or fries. Instead of getting a soggy mess, the air fryer actually crisps up the food you cook, giving it a crunchy and golden surface. To achieve a crispy surface, all you need to do is lightly spray cooking oil over the food. Making anything breaded, as well as any frozen or breaded meal, is best done in this manner.

- **Versatile**

Much more than just a healthy alternative to deep frying, the air fryer has several benefits. In fact, you can prepare almost anything with this gadget, including curries, desserts, whole spaghetti squash, and fried chicken. The hot air convection also roasts, bakes, and cooks food inside the basket.

- **Faster Than Oven Cooking**

Aside from the fact that it heats up more quickly than an oven, an air fryer cooks food more quickly than an oven since it is smaller. In contrast to an oven, which normally requires up to 10 minutes to preheat, the majority of air fryer recipes only require a few seconds to preheat the devices and a few minutes to cook them completely.

How to Set it Up

Start by unboxing your air fryer and checking all of its parts. The parts include a detachable basket with a grate or perforated tray in the bottom. Clean and dry them. Reinstall the basket and grate. Choose an ideal location in your kitchen for your air fryer. Make sure there are at least five inches of space available behind or above the air fryer where the exhaust vent is by keeping your air fryer on a level, heat-resistant surface. Once the air fryer is set, you can plug it in and press the button to turn it on. Your device is now ready to use.

Before you get started with the cooking, make sure to prepare the recipes ahead. It will take a few cooking sessions for you to adjust to the various cooking times, as air fryers can cook your food quickly. When making the perfect bacon, it may just take five minutes to cook in an air fryer, whereas it takes 15 minutes in the oven.

How to Air Fry

Once the air fryer is ready to use, pull the air fryer

drawer out of it and add the food to the air fryer basket. Slide this drawer back into the air fryer and close it. Most air fryers have two common settings, one to set the cooking temperature and the other for the cooking time. You can adjust both manually as per the recipe. Some air fryers come with presets like "fish", "poultry", and "beef", etc. which allow you to select pre-adjusted temperature and time for different categories of food; you can also use these presets to adjust the settings. Once everything is set, you can initiate cooking.

To check for doneness, you can open the air fryer as often as you desire. One of the best features of air fryers is that you may open that drawer as frequently as you'd like to check on the progress of the cooking process. The cooking time of the majority of air fryers won't be affected by this; the fryer stops the timer while you remove the basket and resume cooking when you put it back in. Use toothpicks to secure food. The air fryer's fan occasionally picks up delicate meals and blows them around. So use toothpicks to secure food, such as the top slice of bread on a sandwich.

In order to remove cooked food from the basket, use tongs or a spoon. Your air fryer drawer receives extra oil and drippings during cooking; if you pull the grate out and flip the basket onto a platter, the oil will also run out. This may cause burns, a mess, and greasy food. So, remove the food from the grate and pour the drippings into a separate bowl or throw them away.

Quick Tip: Don't empty the drawer's drippings or cooking liquid after cooking. The juices from the items cooked above and any marinades you pour over the food are both collected in the drawer beneath the air fryer basket. You can use this tasty liquid as a sauce to pour over the dish if the drippings are not overly greasy. To concentrate the flavour, you can also decrease this liquid and reduce it for a short time on the stovetop.

Do you need to add oil to an air fryer?
It goes without saying that you should not use too much oil in an air fryer, and you almost never require more than a tablespoon. Investing in a spray bottle that will enable you to add an evenly distributed layer of oil without going overboard is one of the most popular methods for using oil when air frying. You can rely on the oil that is already present in many dishes, such as bacon or chicken wings, to produce the necessary crisp without the need for additional ingredients.

Getting the Best Out of Air Fryer

Yes, sometimes air-fried meals can turn out to be too dry, too soggy, not so crispy and often half-cooked or over-cooked; this happens when you miss the following little details while cooking. But don't worry, you can avoid those bad results, here is what you need to take care of:

- **Use an Easy-Clean Liner**
To make cleanup simpler, put some parchment paper at the bottom of the basket. For quick cleanup, using foil and parchment paper is fantastic because they both work well in the air fryer! Particularly if you are cooking something that has been marinated. Once you are done cooking, you can simply pull the liner out and throw it away. Just make sure to let it cool first. In this way, the food won't stick to the air fryer basket, and you won't have to scrub hard during cleaning.

- **Always Preheat**
Even though it's not always necessary, this is a great idea when you want to cook a lovely steak with a delicious sear. The secret is to set your cooking temperature as per the recipe instruction and wait 3 minutes to preheat the appliance before adding your food. Some appliances automatically preheat before initiating the timer; if you have one of those air fryers, then you don't have to worry about preheating.

- **Don't Overcrowd the Basket**
Overcrowding the basket keeps the food from browning and crisping and hampers even cooking. Who wants soggy undercooked wings? The hot air has to touch every particle on the surface of the food to make it evenly crisp. Give your food room to spread out as much surface area as you can. By doing that, you can prepare the dish more quickly and with better outcomes.

- **Be Careful with Oil**
Cooking sprays shouldn't be sprayed right into the air

fryer basket. They may harm the non-stick coating inside that basket. An oil mister can be useful in this situation because you can fill it with your own oils, including ones with delightful infusions. And during cooking, when flipping your meal in the basket, you can also use the oil mister to coat it.

- **Hold the Food in Position**

The last thing you want when cooking scallops wrapped in bacon is for the bacon to come undone in the middle of the cooking process. To hold your meal together and in place, feel free to add toothpicks. This helps in preventing food that is extremely light and small from shifting around inside the basket. Cover the food that splatters with a piece of parchment to keep the food particles from blowing during cooking.

- **Shake the Basket and Flip the Food**

Always make sure to flip or shake the food twice or thrice during the entire cooking time of the recipe. By doing this, you can ensure that the skin on both sides will be golden and crisp. Cooking evenly requires shaking a basket, possibly when handling fries, wings, or vegetables, or flipping when handling a larger protein. Nobody wants steaks that are undercooked in some spots while being overdone in others.

- **Don't Let Fatty Foods Produce Smoke**

The air fryer can sometimes produce white smoke, which might be unnerving if you're not sure what's going on. This happens when you cook something fatty inside your fryers, such as bacon or a burger; the fat may start to smoke as it heats up. Adding a light layer of water to the base of your air fryer drawer, which is the space under the basket, is a fantastic way to stop that smoking.

- **Never Hesitate to Accessorize**

One widespread misunderstanding about air fryers is that they may only be used to prepare fried dishes without the need for oil. They can certainly do that, but they are capable of so much more. Another great tip is to use extra accessories that let you get the most out of your air fryer, like the grill pan to make the perfect steak, my favourite, or a baking pan. You can also make pizzas, cakes, and muffins in your air fryer or even silicone moulds to make the perfect frittata or individual cheesy mac and cheese. You will quickly learn that your air fryer is one of the most adaptable kitchen equipment on your counter for just a few extra dollars.

After-Cook Cleaning

After cooking, the hot drawer should not be placed on the counter or other surfaces. Consider the drawer to be a hot pan. It will be hot when you remove it from the appliance, especially the bottom. Take hold of the drawer by the handle, not the other parts, and be prepared to place it down on a trivet or potholder. So every time you are done cooking, allow the drawer and basket to cool down and then wash them.

After each use, wash both the drawer and the basket. Do not put off cleaning the air fryer's drawer because it is incredibly simple to do so. You run the risk of contaminating your food if you don't wash it, and your kitchen will smell awful in a day or two. You can wash the basket and the drawer in the dishwasher (if they are dishwasher safe), or you can use liquid soap and water to wash them. Let the air fryer dry on its own. Simply place the cleaned air fryer drawer and basket inside and turn the appliance on for two to three minutes. That dries both components more effectively than any drying cloth. To clean the exterior of the appliance, simply wipe it off with a clean towel.

CHAPTER 2
Breakfasts

Egg and Bacon Muffins ················· 7

Breakfast Sausage and Cauliflower ········ 7

Simple Cinnamon Toasts ················ 8

Gold Avocado ························ 8

Bacon Eggs on the Go ·················· 9

Pretzels ····························· 9

Banana Bread ························ 10

Parmesan Sausage Egg Muffins ·········· 10

Super Easy Bacon Cups ················ 11

Posh Orange Rolls ···················· 11

Egg and Bacon Muffins

SERVES 1

| PREP TIME: 5 minutes
| COOK TIME: 15 minutes

2 eggs
Salt and ground black pepper, to taste
1 tbsp. green pesto
85 g shredded Cheddar cheese
142 g cooked bacon
1 spring onion, chopped

1. Preheat the air fryer to 180ºC. Line a cupcake tin with parchment paper.
2. Beat the eggs with pepper, salt, and pesto in a bowl. Mix in the cheese.
3. Pour the eggs into the cupcake tin and top with the bacon and spring onion.
4. Bake in the preheated air fryer for 15 minutes, or until the egg is set.
5. Serve immediately.

Breakfast Sausage and Cauliflower

SERVES 4

| PREP TIME: 5 minutes
| COOK TIME: 45 minutes

454 g sausage, cooked and crumbled
480 g heavy whipping cream
1 head cauliflower, chopped
80 g grated Cheddar cheese, plus more for topping
8 eggs, beaten
Salt and ground black pepper, to taste

1. Preheat the air fryer to 180ºC.
2. In a large bowl, mix the sausage, heavy whipping cream, chopped cauliflower, cheese and eggs. Sprinkle with salt and ground black pepper.
3. Pour the mixture into a greased casserole dish. Bake in the preheated air fryer for 45 minutes or until firm.
4. Top with more Cheddar cheese and serve.

Simple Cinnamon Toasts

SERVES 4

| PREP TIME: 5 minutes
| COOK TIME: 4 minutes

1 tbsp. salted butter
2 tsps. ground cinnamon
4 tbsps. sugar
½ tsp. vanilla extract
10 bread slices

1. Preheat the air fryer to 195ºC.
2. In a bowl, combine the butter, cinnamon, sugar, and vanilla extract. Spread onto the slices of bread.
3. Put the bread inside the air fryer and bake for 4 minutes or until golden brown.
4. Serve warm.

Gold Avocado

SERVES 4

| PREP TIME: 5 minutes
| COOK TIME: 6 minutes

2 large avocados, sliced
¼ tsp. paprika
Salt and ground black pepper, to taste
60 g flour
2 eggs, beaten
120 g bread crumbs

1. Preheat the air fryer to 205ºC.
2. Sprinkle paprika, salt and pepper on the slices of avocado.
3. Lightly coat the avocados with flour. Dredge them in the eggs, before covering with bread crumbs.
4. Transfer to the air fryer and air fry for 6 minutes.
5. Serve warm.

CHAPTER 2
Breakfasts

Bacon Eggs on the Go

SERVES 1

| PREP TIME: 5 minutes
| COOK TIME: 15 minutes

2 eggs
115 g bacon, cooked
Salt and ground black pepper, to taste

1. Preheat the air fryer to 205ºC. Put liners in a regular cupcake tin.
2. Crack an egg into each of the cups and add the bacon. Season with some pepper and salt.
3. Bake in the preheated air fryer for 15 minutes, or until the eggs are set.
4. Serve warm.

Pretzels

MAKES 24 PRETZELS

| PREP TIME: 10 minutes
| COOK TIME: 6 minutes

2 tsps. yeast
240 ml water, warm
1 tsp. sugar
1 tsp. salt
310 g plain flour

2 tbsps. butter, melted, plus more as needed
240 ml boiling water
1 tbsp. baking soda
Coarse sea salt, to taste

1. Combine the yeast and water in a small bowl. Combine the sugar, salt and flour in the bowl of a stand mixer. With the mixer running and using the dough hook, drizzle in the yeast mixture and melted butter and knead dough until smooth and elastic, about 10 minutes. Shape into a ball and let the dough rise for 1 hour.
2. Punch the dough down to release any air and divide the dough into 24 portions.
3. Roll each portion into a skinny rope using both hands on the counter and rolling from the centre to the ends of the rope. Spin the rope into a pretzel shape (or tie the rope into a knot) and place the tied pretzels on a parchment lined baking sheet.
4. Preheat the air fryer to 180ºC.
5. Combine the boiling water and baking soda in a shallow bowl and whisk to dissolve. Let the water cool so you can put the hands in it. Working in batches, dip the pretzels (top side down) into the baking soda mixture and let them soak for 30 seconds to a minute. Then remove the pretzels carefully and return them (top side up) to the baking sheet. Sprinkle the coarse salt on the top.
6. Air fry in batches for 3 minutes per side. When the pretzels are finished, brush them generously with the melted butter and enjoy them warm.

Banana Bread

MAKES 3 LOAVES

| **PREP TIME:** 10 minutes
| **COOK TIME:** 22 minutes

3 ripe bananas, mashed
200 g sugar
1 large egg
4 tbsps. unsalted butter, melted
190 g plain flour
1 tsp. baking soda
1 tsp. salt

1. Coat the insides of 3 mini loaf pans with cooking spray.
2. In a large mixing bowl, mix the bananas and sugar.
3. In a separate large mixing bowl, combine the egg, butter, flour, baking soda, and salt and mix well.
4. Add the banana mixture to the egg and flour mixture. Mix well.
5. Divide the batter evenly among the prepared pans.
6. Preheat the air fryer to 155ºC. Set the mini loaf pans into the air fryer basket.
7. Bake in the preheated air fryer for 22 minutes. Insert a toothpick into the centre of each loaf; if it comes out clean, they are done.
8. When the loaves are cooked through, remove the pans from the air fryer basket. Turn out the loaves onto a wire rack to cool.
9. Serve warm.

Parmesan Sausage Egg Muffins

SERVES 4

| **PREP TIME:** 5 minutes
| **COOK TIME:** 20 minutes

170 g Italian sausage, sliced
6 eggs
30 g heavy cream
Salt and ground black pepper, to taste
85 g Parmesan cheese, grated

1. Preheat the air fryer to 180ºC. Grease a muffin pan.
2. Put the sliced sausage in the muffin pan.
3. Beat the eggs with the cream in a bowl and season with salt and pepper.
4. Pour half of the mixture over the sausages in the pan.
5. Sprinkle with cheese and the remaining egg mixture.
6. Bake in the preheated air fryer for 20 minutes or until set.
7. Serve immediately.

Super Easy Bacon Cups

SERVES 2

| PREP TIME: 5 minutes
| COOK TIME: 20 minutes

3 slices bacon, cooked, sliced in half
2 slices ham
1 slice tomato
2 eggs
2 tsps. grated Parmesan cheese
Salt and ground black pepper, to taste

1. Preheat the air fryer to 190ºC. Line 2 greased muffin tins with 3 half-strips of bacon.
2. Put one slice of ham and half slice of tomato in each muffin tin on top of the bacon.
3. Crack one egg on top of the tomato in each muffin tin and sprinkle each with half a tsp. of grated Parmesan cheese. Sprinkle with salt and ground black pepper, if desired.
4. Bake in the preheated air fryer for 20 minutes. Remove from the air fryer and let cool.
5. Serve warm.

Posh Orange Rolls

MAKES 8 ROLLS

| PREP TIME: 15 minutes
| COOK TIME: 8 minutes

85 g low-fat cream cheese
1 tbsp. low-fat sour cream or plain yogurt
2 tsps. sugar
¼ tsp. pure vanilla extract
¼ tsp. orange extract
1 can organic crescent roll dough
40 g chopped walnuts
30 g dried cranberries
20 g desiccated, sweetened coconut
Butter-flavoured cooking spray
Orange Glaze:
65 g icing sugar
1 tbsp. orange juice
¼ tsp. orange extract
Dash of salt

1. Cut a circular piece of parchment paper slightly smaller than the bottom of the air fryer basket. Set aside.
2. In a small bowl, combine the cream cheese, sour cream or yogurt, sugar, and vanilla and orange extracts. Stir until smooth.
3. Preheat the air fryer to 150ºC.
4. Separate crescent roll dough into 8 triangles and divide cream cheese mixture among them. Starting at wide end, spread cheese mixture to within 2-cm of point.
5. Sprinkle nuts and cranberries evenly over cheese mixture.
6. Starting at wide end, roll up triangles, then sprinkle with coconut, pressing in lightly to make it stick. Spray tops of rolls with butter-flavoured cooking spray.
7. Put parchment paper in air fryer basket, and place 4 rolls on top, spaced evenly.
8. Air fry for 8 minutes, until rolls are golden brown and cooked through.
9. Repeat steps 7 and 8 to air fry remaining 4 rolls. You should be able to use the same piece of parchment paper twice.
10. In a small bowl, stir together ingredients for glaze and drizzle over warm rolls. Serve warm.

CHAPTER 3
Vegetables

Russet Potato Gratin · 13

Ratatouille · 13

Potato with Creamy Cheese · · · · · · · · · · · · · · 14

Roasted Potatoes and Asparagus · · · · · · · · · 14

Sesame Taj Tofu · 15

Chili Fingerling Potatoes · · · · · · · · · · · · · · · · · 15

Tofu Bites · 16

Ricotta Potatoes · 16

Sweet Potatoes with Courgette · · · · · · · · · · · 17

Super Veg Rolls · 17

Potato and Broccoli with Tofu Scramble   18

Cracker Wax Beans · 18

Lush Vegetables Roast · · · · · · · · · · · · · · · · · · 18

Russet Potato Gratin

SERVES 6

| **PREP TIME:** 10 minutes
| **COOK TIME:** 35 minutes

120 ml milk
7 medium russet potatoes, peeled
Salt, to taste
1 tsp. black pepper
120 g heavy whipping cream
40 g grated semi-mature cheese
½ tsp. nutmeg

1. Preheat the air fryer to 200ºC.
2. Cut the potatoes into wafer-thin slices.
3. In a bowl, combine the milk and cream and sprinkle with salt, pepper, and nutmeg.
4. Use the milk mixture to coat the slices of potatoes. Put in a baking dish. Top the potatoes with the rest of the milk mixture.
5. Put the baking dish into the air fryer basket and bake for 25 minutes.
6. Pour the cheese over the potatoes.
7. Bake for an additional 10 minutes, ensuring the top is nicely browned before serving.

Ratatouille

SERVES 4

| **PREP TIME:** 20 minutes
| **COOK TIME:** 25 minutes

1 sprig basil
1 sprig flat-leaf parsley
1 sprig mint
1 tbsp. coriander powder
1 tsp. capers
½ lemon, juiced
Salt and ground black pepper, to taste
2 aubergines, sliced crosswise
2 red onions, chopped
4 cloves garlic, minced
2 red peppers, sliced crosswise
1 fennel bulb, sliced crosswise
3 large courgettes, sliced crosswise
5 tbsps. olive oil
4 large tomatoes, chopped
2 tsps. herbs de Provence

1. Blend the basil, parsley, coriander, mint, lemon juice and capers, with a little salt and pepper. Make sure all ingredients are well-incorporated.
2. Preheat the air fryer to 200ºC.
3. Coat the aubergine, onions, garlic, peppers, fennel, and courgette with olive oil.
4. Transfer the vegetables into a baking dish and top with the tomatoes and herb purée. Sprinkle with more salt and pepper, and the herbs de Provence.
5. Air fry for 25 minutes.
6. Serve immediately.

Potato with Creamy Cheese

SERVES 2

| PREP TIME: 5 minutes
| COOK TIME: 15 minutes

2 medium potatoes
1 tsp. butter
3 tbsps. sour cream
1 tsp. chives
1½ tbsps. grated Parmesan cheese

1. Preheat the air fryer to 180ºC.
2. Pierce the potatoes with a fork and boil them in water until they are cooked.
3. Transfer to the air fryer and air fry for 15 minutes.
4. In the meantime, combine the sour cream, cheese and chives in a bowl. Cut the potatoes halfway to open them up and fill with the butter and sour cream mixture.
5. Serve immediately.

Roasted Potatoes and Asparagus

SERVES 4

| PREP TIME: 5 minutes
| COOK TIME: 23 minutes

4 medium potatoes
1 bunch asparagus
78 g cottage cheese
85 g low-fat crème fraiche
1 tbsp. wholegrain mustard
Salt and pepper, to taste
Cook spray

1. Preheat the air fryer to 200ºC. Spritz the air fryer basket with cooking spray.
2. Place the potatoes in the basket. Air fry the potatoes for 20 minutes.
3. Boil the asparagus in salted water for 3 minutes.
4. Remove the potatoes and mash them with rest of ingredients. Sprinkle with salt and pepper.
5. Serve immediately.

CHAPTER 3
Vegetables

Sesame Taj Tofu

SERVES 4

PREP TIME: 5 minutes
COOK TIME: 25 minutes

1 block firm tofu, pressed and cut into 2-cm thick cubes
2 tbsps. soy sauce
2 tsps. toasted sesame seeds
1 tsp. rice vinegar
1 tbsp. cornflour

1. Preheat the air fryer to 200ºC.
2. Add the tofu, soy sauce, sesame seeds, and rice vinegar in a bowl together and mix well to coat the tofu cubes. Then cover the tofu in cornflour and put it in the air fryer basket.
3. Air fry for 25 minutes, giving the basket a shake at five-minute intervals to ensure the tofu cooks evenly.
4. Serve immediately.

Chili Fingerling Potatoes

SERVES 4

PREP TIME: 10 minutes
COOK TIME: 16 minutes

454 g fingerling potatoes, rinsed and cut into wedges
1 tsp. olive oil
1 tsp. salt
1 tsp. black pepper
1 tsp. cayenne pepper
1 tsp. nutritional yeast
½ tsp. garlic powder

1. Preheat the air fryer to 200ºC.
2. Coat the potatoes with the rest of the ingredients.
3. Transfer to the air fryer basket and air fry for 16 minutes, shaking the basket at the halfway point.
4. Serve immediately.

CHAPTER 3
Vegetables

Tofu Bites

SERVES 4

| **PREP TIME:** 15 minutes
| **COOK TIME:** 30 minutes

1 packaged firm tofu, cubed and pressed to remove excess water
1 tbsp. soy sauce
1 tbsp. ketchup
1 tbsp. maple syrup
½ tsp. vinegar
1 tsp. liquid smoke
1 tsp. hot sauce
2 tbsps. sesame seeds
1 tsp. garlic powder
Salt and ground black pepper, to taste
Cooking spray

1. Preheat the air fryer to 190ºC.
2. Spritz a baking dish with cooking spray.
3. Combine all the ingredients to coat the tofu completely and allow the marinade to absorb for half an hour.
4. Transfer the tofu to the baking dish, then air fry for 15 minutes. Flip the tofu over and air fry for another 15 minutes on the other side.
5. Serve immediately.

Ricotta Potatoes

SERVES 4

| **PREP TIME:** 15 minutes
| **COOK TIME:** 15 minutes

4 potatoes
2 tbsps. olive oil
115 g Ricotta cheese, at room temperature
2 tbsps. chopped spring onions
1 tbsp. roughly chopped fresh parsley
1 tbsp. minced coriander
57 g Cheddar cheese, preferably freshly grated
1 tsp. celery seeds
½ tsp. salt
½ tsp. garlic pepper

1. Preheat the air fryer to 180ºC.
2. Pierce the skin of the potatoes with a knife.
3. Air fry in the air fryer basket for 13 minutes. If they are not cooked through by this time, leave for 2 to 3 minutes longer.
4. In the meantime, make the stuffing by combining all the other ingredients.
5. Cut halfway into the cooked potatoes to open them.
6. Spoon equal amounts of the stuffing into each potato and serve hot.

CHAPTER 3
Vegetables

Sweet Potatoes with Courgette

SERVES 4

PREP TIME: 20 minutes **COOK TIME:** 20 minutes	2 large-sized sweet potatoes, peeled and quartered 1 medium courgette, sliced 1 Serrano pepper, deseeded and thinly sliced 1 pepper, deseeded and thinly sliced 1 to 2 carrots, cut into matchsticks 60 ml olive oil 1½ tbsps. maple syrup ½ tsp. porcini powder ¼ tsp. mustard powder ½ tsp. fennel seeds 1 tbsp. garlic powder ½ tsp. fine sea salt ¼ tsp. ground black pepper Tomato ketchup, for serving

1. Put the sweet potatoes, courgette, peppers, and the carrot into the air fryer basket. Coat with a drizzling of olive oil.
2. Preheat the air fryer to 180°C.
3. Air fry the vegetables for 15 minutes.
4. In the meantime, prepare the sauce by vigorously combining the other ingredients, except for the tomato ketchup, with a whisk.
5. Lightly grease a baking dish.
6. Transfer the cooked vegetables to the baking dish, pour over the sauce and coat the vegetables well.
7. Increase the temperature to 200°C and air fry the vegetables for an additional 5 minutes.
8. Serve warm with a side of ketchup.

Super Veg Rolls

SERVES 6

PREP TIME: 20 minutes **COOK TIME:** 10 minutes	2 potatoes, mashed 30 g peas 40 g mashed carrots 1 small cabbage, sliced 45 g beans 2 tbsps. sweetcorn 1 small onion, chopped 60 g bread crumbs 1 packet spring roll sheets 60 g cornflour slurry

1. Preheat the air fryer to 200°C.
2. Boil all the vegetables in water over a low heat. Rinse and allow to dry.
3. Unroll the spring roll sheets and spoon equal amounts of vegetable onto the centre of each one. Fold into spring rolls and coat each one with the slurry and bread crumbs.
4. Air fry the rolls in the preheated air fryer for 10 minutes.
5. Serve warm.

Potato and Broccoli with Tofu Scramble

SERVES 3

| PREP TIME: 15 minutes
| COOK TIME: 30 minutes

350 g chopped red potato
2 tbsps. olive oil, divided
1 block tofu, chopped finely
2 tbsps. tamari
1 tsp. turmeric powder

½ tsp. onion powder
½ tsp. garlic powder
30 g chopped onion
285 g broccoli florets

1. Preheat the air fryer to 200ºC.
2. Toss together the potatoes and 1 tbsp. of the olive oil.
3. Air fry the potatoes in a baking dish for 15 minutes, shaking once during the cooking time to ensure they fry evenly.
4. Combine the tofu, the remaining 1 tbsp. of the olive oil, turmeric, onion powder, tamari, and garlic powder together, stirring in the onions, followed by the broccoli.
5. Top the potatoes with the tofu mixture and air fry for an additional 15 minutes. Serve warm.

Cracker Wax Beans

SERVES 4

| PREP TIME: 10 minutes
| COOK TIME: 7 minutes

65 g flour
1 tsp. smoky chipotle powder
½ tsp. ground black pepper
1 tsp. sea salt flakes

2 eggs, beaten
57 g crushed cream crackers
283 g wax beans
Cooking spray

1. Preheat the air fryer to 180ºC.
2. Combine the flour, chipotle powder, black pepper, and salt in a bowl. Put the eggs in a second bowl. Put the crushed crackers in a third bowl.
3. Wash the beans with cold water and discard any tough strings.
4. Coat the beans with the flour mixture, before dipping them into the beaten egg. Cover them with the crushed saltines.
5. Spritz the beans with cooking spray.
6. Air fry for 4 minutes. Give the air fryer basket a good shake and continue to air fry for 3 minutes. Serve hot.

Lush Vegetables Roast

SERVES 6

| PREP TIME: 15 minutes
| COOK TIME: 20 minutes

180 g small parsnips, peeled and cubed
130 g celery
2 red onions, sliced
180 g small butternut squash, cut in half, deseeded and cubed
1 tbsp. fresh thyme needles
1 tbsp. olive oil
Salt and ground black pepper, to taste

1. Preheat the air fryer to 200ºC.
2. Combine the cut vegetables with the thyme, olive oil, salt and pepper.
3. Put the vegetables in the basket and transfer the basket to the air fryer.
4. Roast for 20 minutes, stirring once throughout the roasting time, until the vegetables are nicely browned and cooked through.
5. Serve warm.

CHAPTER 4
Poultry

Almond-Crusted Chicken Nuggets·········20

Cranberry Curry Chicken·····················20

Jerk Chicken Leg Quarters····················21

Air Fryer Chicken Fajitas······················21

Barbecue Chicken·······························22

Whole Chicken Roast···························22

Garlic Soy Chicken Thighs····················23

Apricot-Glazed Chicken······················23

Roasted Chicken and Vegetable Salad····24

Lemon Chicken and Spinach Salad········24

Easy Tandoori Chicken························25

Chicken with Pineapple and Peach········25

Tex-Mex Chicken Breasts····················26

Curried Orange Honey Chicken············26

Buttermilk Paprika Chicken··················27

Roasted Chicken with Garlic················27

Lemon Garlic Chicken························28

Chicken Manchurian··························28

Almond-Crusted Chicken Nuggets

SERVES 4

| PREP TIME: 10 minutes
| COOK TIME: 10-13 minutes

1 egg white
1 tbsp. freshly squeezed lemon juice
½ tsp. dried basil
½ tsp. ground paprika
454 g low-sodium boneless, skinless chicken breasts, cut into 3-cm cubes
58 g ground almonds
2 slices low-sodium whole-wheat bread, crumbled

1. Preheat the air fryer to 200ºC.
2. In a shallow bowl, beat the egg white, lemon juice, basil, and paprika with a fork until foamy.
3. Add the chicken and stir to coat.
4. On a plate, mix the almonds and bread crumbs.
5. Toss the chicken cubes in the almond and bread crumb mixture until coated.
6. Bake the nuggets in the air fryer, in two batches, for 10 to 13 minutes, or until the chicken reaches an internal temperature of 75ºC on a meat thermometer. Serve immediately.

Cranberry Curry Chicken

SERVES 4

| PREP TIME: 12 minutes
| COOK TIME: 18 minutes

3 (142-g) low-sodium boneless, skinless chicken breasts, cut into 3-cm cubes
2 tsps. olive oil
2 tbsps. cornflour
1 tbsp. curry powder
1 tart apple, chopped
120 ml low-sodium chicken stock
40 g dried cranberries
2 tbsps. freshly squeezed orange juice
Brown rice, cooked (optional)

1. Preheat the air fryer to 190ºC.
2. In a medium bowl, mix the chicken and olive oil. Sprinkle with the cornflour and curry powder. Toss to coat. Stir in the apple and transfer to a metal pan. Bake in the air fryer for 8 minutes, stirring once during cooking.
3. Add the chicken stock, cranberries, and orange juice. Bake for about 10 minutes more, or until the sauce is slightly thickened and the chicken reaches an internal temperature of 75ºC on a meat thermometer. Serve over hot cooked brown rice, if desired.

Jerk Chicken Leg Quarters

SERVES 2

PREP TIME: 8 minutes
COOK TIME: 27 minutes

1 tbsp. packed brown sugar
1 tsp. ground allspice
1 tsp. pepper
1 tsp. garlic powder
¾ tsp. dry mustard
¾ tsp. dried thyme
½ tsp. salt
¼ tsp. cayenne pepper
2 (284-g) chicken leg quarters, trimmed
1 tsp. vegetable oil
1 spring onion, green part only, sliced thin
Lime wedges

1. Preheat the air fryer to 200ºC.
2. Combine sugar, allspice, pepper, garlic powder, mustard, thyme, salt, and cayenne in a bowl. Pat chicken dry with paper towels. Using metal skewer, poke 10 to 15 holes in skin of each chicken leg. Rub with oil and sprinkle evenly with spice mixture.
3. Arrange chicken skin-side up in the air fryer basket, spaced evenly apart. Air fry until chicken is well browned and crisp, 27 to 30 minutes, rotating chicken halfway through cooking (do not flip).
4. Transfer chicken to plate, tent loosely with aluminum foil, and let rest for 5 minutes. Sprinkle with spring onion. Serve with lime wedges.

Air Fryer Chicken Fajitas

SERVES 4

PREP TIME: 15 minutes
COOK TIME: 10-15 minutes

4 (142-g) low-sodium boneless, skinless chicken breasts, cut into 8- by-1-cm strips
1 tbsp. freshly squeezed lemon juice
2 tsps. olive oil
2 tsps. chili powder
2 red peppers, sliced
4 low-sodium whole-wheat tortillas
80 g nonfat sour cream
210 g grape tomatoes, sliced

1. Preheat the air fryer to 190ºC.
2. In a large bowl, mix the chicken, lemon juice, olive oil, and chili powder. Toss to coat. Transfer the chicken to the air fryer basket. Add the red peppers. Roast for 10 to 15 minutes, or until the chicken reaches an internal temperature of 75ºC on a meat thermometer.
3. Assemble the fajitas with the tortillas, chicken, peppers, sour cream, and tomatoes. Serve immediately.

Barbecue Chicken

SERVES 4

| PREP TIME: 10 minutes
| COOK TIME: 18-20 minutes

80 g no-salt-added tomato sauce
2 tbsps. low-sodium grainy mustard
2 tbsps. apple cider vinegar
1 tbsp. honey
2 garlic cloves, minced
1 jalapeño pepper, minced
3 tbsps. minced onion
4 (142-g) low-sodium boneless, skinless chicken breasts

1. Preheat the air fryer to 190ºC.
2. In a small bowl, stir together the tomato sauce, mustard, cider vinegar, honey, garlic, jalapeño, and onion.
3. Brush the chicken breasts with some sauce and air fry for 10 minutes.
4. Remove the air fryer basket and turn the chicken; brush with more sauce. Air fry for 5 minutes more.
5. Remove the air fryer basket and turn the chicken again; brush with more sauce. Air fry for 3 to 5 minutes more, or until the chicken reaches an internal temperature of 75ºC on a meat thermometer. Discard any remaining sauce. Serve immediately.

Whole Chicken Roast

SERVES 6

| PREP TIME: 10 minutes
| COOK TIME: 1 hour

1 tsp. salt
1 tsp. Italian seasoning
½ tsp. freshly ground black pepper
½ tsp. paprika
½ tsp. garlic powder
½ tsp. onion powder
2 tbsps. olive oil, plus more as needed
1 (1.8-kg) fryer chicken

1. Preheat the air fryer to 180ºC.
2. Grease the air fryer basket lightly with olive oil.
3. In a small bowl, mix the salt, Italian seasoning, pepper, paprika, garlic powder, and onion powder.
4. Remove any giblets from the chicken. Pat the chicken dry thoroughly with paper towels, including the cavity.
5. Brush the chicken all over with the olive oil and rub it with the seasoning mixture.
6. Truss the chicken or tie the legs with butcher's twine. This will make it easier to flip the chicken during cooking.
7. Put the chicken in the air fryer basket, breast-side down. Air fry for 30 minutes. Flip the chicken over and baste it with any drippings collected in the bottom drawer of the air fryer. Lightly brush the chicken with olive oil.
8. Air fry for 20 minutes. Flip the chicken over one last time and air fry until a thermometer inserted into the thickest part of the thigh reaches at least 74ºC and it's crispy and golden, 10 more minutes. Continue to cook, checking every 5 minutes until the chicken reaches the correct internal temperature.
9. Let the chicken rest for 10 minutes before carving and serving.

CHAPTER 4
Poultry

Garlic Soy Chicken Thighs

SERVES 1-2

| **PREP TIME:** 10 minutes
| **COOK TIME:** 30 minutes

2 tbsps. chicken stock
2 tbsps. reduced-sodium soy sauce
1½ tbsps. sugar
4 garlic cloves, smashed and peeled
2 large spring onions, cut into 4- to 6-cm batons, plus more, thinly sliced, for garnish
2 bone-in, skin-on chicken thighs (198 to 227 g each)

1. Preheat the air fryer to 190°C.
2. In a metal cake pan, combine the chicken stock, soy sauce, and sugar and stir until the sugar dissolves. Add the garlic cloves, spring onions, and chicken thighs, turning the thighs to coat them in the marinade, then resting them skin-side up. Place the pan in the air fryer and bake, flipping the thighs every 5 minutes after the first 10 minutes, until the chicken is cooked through and the marinade is reduced to a sticky glaze over the chicken, about 30 minutes.
3. Remove the pan from the air fryer and serve the chicken thighs warm, with any remaining glaze spooned over top and sprinkled with more sliced spring onions.

Apricot-Glazed Chicken

SERVES 2

| **PREP TIME:** 5 minutes
| **COOK TIME:** 12 minutes

2 tbsps. apricot preserves
½ tsp. minced fresh thyme or ⅛ tsp. dried
2 (227-g) boneless, skinless chicken breasts, trimmed
1 tsp. vegetable oil
Salt and pepper, to taste

1. Preheat the air fryer to 200°C.
2. Microwave apricot preserves and thyme in bowl until fluid, about 30 seconds; set aside. Pound chicken to uniform thickness as needed. Pat dry with paper towels, rub with oil, and season with salt and pepper.
3. Arrange breasts skin-side down in air fryer basket, spaced evenly apart, alternating ends. Air fry the chicken for 4 minutes. Flip chicken and brush skin side with apricot-thyme mixture. Air fry until chicken registers 70°C, 8 to 12 minutes more.
4. Transfer chicken to serving platter, tent loosely with aluminum foil, and let rest for 5 minutes. Serve.

Roasted Chicken and Vegetable Salad

SERVES 4

| PREP TIME: 10 minutes
| COOK TIME: 10-13 minutes

3 (113-g) low-sodium boneless, skinless chicken breasts, cut into 2-cm cubes
1 small red onion, sliced
1 red pepper, sliced
133 g green beans, cut into 2-cm pieces
2 tbsps. low-fat ranch salad dressing
2 tbsps. freshly squeezed lemon juice
½ tsp. dried basil
40 g mixed lettuce

1. Preheat the air fryer to 200°C.
2. In the air fryer basket, roast the chicken, red onion, red pepper, and green beans for 10 to 13 minutes, or until the chicken reaches an internal temperature of 75°C on a meat thermometer, tossing the food in the basket once during cooking.
3. While the chicken cooks, in a serving bowl, mix the ranch dressing, lemon juice, and basil.
4. Transfer the chicken and vegetables to a serving bowl and toss with the dressing to coat. Serve immediately on lettuce leaves.

Lemon Chicken and Spinach Salad

SERVES 4

| PREP TIME: 10 minutes
| COOK TIME: 16-20 minutes

3 (142-g) low-sodium boneless, skinless chicken breasts, cut into 2-cm cubes
5 tsps. olive oil
½ tsp. dried thyme
1 medium red onion, sliced
1 red pepper, sliced
1 small courgette, cut into strips
3 tbsps. freshly squeezed lemon juice
50 g fresh baby spinach

1. Preheat the air fryer to 200°C.
2. In a large bowl, mix the chicken with the olive oil and thyme. Toss to coat. Transfer to a medium metal bowl and roast for 8 minutes in the air fryer.
3. Add the red onion, red pepper, and courgette. Roast for 8 to 12 minutes more, stirring once during cooking, or until the chicken reaches an internal temperature of 75°C on a meat thermometer.
4. Remove the bowl from the air fryer and stir in the lemon juice.
5. Put the spinach in a serving bowl and top with the chicken mixture. Toss to combine and serve immediately.

Easy Tandoori Chicken

SERVES 4

| PREP TIME: 5 minutes
| COOK TIME: 18-23 minutes

171 g plain low-fat yogurt
2 tbsps. freshly squeezed lemon juice
2 tsps. curry powder
½ tsp. ground cinnamon
2 garlic cloves, minced
2 tsps. olive oil
4 (142-g) low-sodium boneless, skinless chicken breasts

1. In a medium bowl, whisk the yogurt, lemon juice, curry powder, cinnamon, garlic, and olive oil.
2. With a sharp knife, cut thin slashes into the chicken. Add it to the yogurt mixture and turn to coat. Let stand for 10 minutes at room temperature. You can also prepare this ahead of time and marinate the chicken in the refrigerator for up to 24 hours.
3. Preheat the air fryer to 180ºC.
4. Remove the chicken from the marinade and shake off any excess liquid. Discard any remaining marinade.
5. Roast the chicken for 10 minutes. With tongs, carefully turn each piece. Roast for 8 to 13 minutes more, or until the chicken reaches an internal temperature of 75ºC on a meat thermometer. Serve immediately.

Chicken with Pineapple and Peach

SERVES 4

| PREP TIME: 10 minutes
| COOK TIME: 14-15 minutes

454 g low-sodium boneless, skinless chicken breasts, cut into 2-cm pieces
1 medium red onion, chopped
1 (227-g) can pineapple chunks, drained, 60-ml juice reserved
1 tbsp. peanut oil or safflower oil
1 peach, peeled, pitted, and cubed
1 tbsp. cornflour
½ tsp. ground ginger
¼ tsp. ground allspice
Brown rice, cooked (optional)

1. Preheat the air fryer to 190ºC.
2. In a medium metal bowl, mix the chicken, red onion, pineapple, and peanut oil. Bake in the air fryer for 9 minutes. Remove and stir.
3. Add the peach and return the bowl to the air fryer. Bake for 3 minutes more. Remove and stir again.
4. In a small bowl, whisk the reserved pineapple juice, the cornflour, ginger, and allspice well. Add to the chicken mixture and stir to combine.
5. Bake for 2 to 3 minutes more, or until the chicken reaches an internal temperature of 75C on a meat thermometer and the sauce is slightly thickened.
6. Serve immediately over hot cooked brown rice, if desired.

Tex-Mex Chicken Breasts

SERVES 4

| **PREP TIME:** 10 minutes
| **COOK TIME:** 17-20 minutes

454 g low-sodium boneless, skinless chicken breasts, cut into 2-cm cubes
1 medium onion, chopped
1 red pepper, chopped
1 jalapeño pepper, minced
2 tsps. olive oil
83 g canned low-sodium black beans, rinsed and drained
125 g low-sodium salsa
2 tsps. chili powder

1. Preheat the air fryer to 200ºC.
2. In a medium metal bowl, mix the chicken, onion, pepper, jalapeño, and olive oil. Roast for 10 minutes, stirring once during cooking.
3. Add the black beans, salsa, and chili powder. Roast for 7 to 10 minutes more, stirring once, until the chicken reaches an internal temperature of 75ºC on a meat thermometer. Serve immediately.

Curried Orange Honey Chicken

SERVES 4

| **PREP TIME:** 10 minutes
| **COOK TIME:** 16-19 minutes

340 g boneless, skinless chicken thighs, cut into 2-cm pieces
1 yellow pepper, cut into 3-cm pieces
1 small red onion, sliced
Olive oil for misting
60 ml chicken stock
2 tbsps. honey
60 ml orange juice
1 tbsp. cornflour
2 to 3 tsps. curry powder

1. Preheat the air fryer to 190ºC.
2. Put the chicken thighs, pepper, and red onion in the air fryer basket and mist with olive oil.
3. Roast for 12 to 14 minutes or until the chicken is cooked to 75ºC, shaking the basket halfway through cooking time.
4. Remove the chicken and vegetables from the air fryer basket and set aside.
5. In a metal bowl, combine the stock, honey, orange juice, cornflour, and curry powder, and mix well. Add the chicken and vegetables, stir, and put the bowl in the basket.
6. Return the basket to the air fryer and roast for 2 minutes. Remove and stir, then roast for 2 to 3 minutes or until the sauce is thickened and bubbly.
7. Serve warm.

Buttermilk Paprika Chicken

SERVES 4

| PREP TIME: 7 minutes
| COOK TIME: 17-23 minutes

4 (142-g) low-sodium boneless, skinless chicken breasts, pounded to about 1-cm thick
120 ml buttermilk
65 g plain flour
2 tbsps. cornflour
1 tsp. dried thyme
1 tsp. ground paprika
1 egg white
1 tbsp. olive oil

1. Preheat the air fryer to 200ºC.
2. In a shallow bowl, mix the chicken and buttermilk. Let stand for 10 minutes.
3. Meanwhile, in another shallow bowl, mix the flour, cornflour, thyme, and paprika.
4. In a small bowl, whisk the egg white and olive oil. Quickly stir this egg mixture into the flour mixture so the dry ingredients are evenly moistened.
5. Remove the chicken from the buttermilk and shake off any excess liquid. Dip each piece of chicken into the flour mixture to coat.
6. Air fry the chicken in the air fryer basket for 17 to 23 minutes, or until the chicken reaches an internal temperature of 75ºC on a meat thermometer. Serve immediately.

Roasted Chicken with Garlic

SERVES 4

| PREP TIME: 5 minutes
| COOK TIME: 25 minutes

4 (142-g) low-sodium bone-in skinless chicken breasts
1 tbsp. olive oil
1 tbsp. freshly squeezed lemon juice
3 tbsps. cornflour
1 tsp. dried basil leaves
⅛ tsp. freshly ground black pepper
20 garlic cloves, unpeeled

1. Preheat the air fryer to 190ºC.
2. Rub the chicken with the olive oil and lemon juice on both sides and sprinkle with the cornflour, basil, and pepper.
3. Place the seasoned chicken in the air fryer basket and top with the garlic cloves. Roast for about 25 minutes, or until the garlic is soft and the chicken reaches an internal temperature of 75ºC on a meat thermometer. Serve immediately.

Lemon Garlic Chicken

SERVES 4

| PREP TIME: 10 minutes
| COOK TIME: 16-19 minutes

4 (142-g) low-sodium boneless, skinless chicken breasts, cut into 8-by-1-cm strips
2 tsps. olive oil
2 tbsps. cornflour
3 garlic cloves, minced
120 ml low-sodium chicken stock
60 ml freshly squeezed lemon juice
1 tbsp. honey
½ tsp. dried thyme
Brown rice, cooked (optional)

1. Preheat the air fryer to 200°C.
2. In a large bowl, mix the chicken and olive oil. Sprinkle with the cornflour. Toss to coat.
3. Add the garlic and transfer to a metal pan. Bake in the air fryer for 10 minutes, stirring once during cooking.
4. Add the chicken stock, lemon juice, honey, and thyme to the chicken mixture. Bake for 6 to 9 minutes more, or until the sauce is slightly thickened and the chicken reaches an internal temperature of 75°C on a meat thermometer. Serve over hot cooked brown rice, if desired.

Chicken Manchurian

SERVES 2

| PREP TIME: 10 minutes
| COOK TIME: 20 minutes

454 g boneless, skinless chicken breasts, cut into 2-cm pieces
62 g ketchup
1 tbsp. tomato-based chili sauce, such as Heinz
1 tbsp. soy sauce
1 tbsp. rice vinegar
2 tsps. vegetable oil
1 tsp. hot sauce, such as Tabasco
½ tsp. garlic powder
¼ tsp. cayenne pepper
2 spring onions, thinly sliced
Cooked white rice, for serving

1. Preheat the air fryer to 180°C.
2. In a bowl, combine the chicken, ketchup, chili sauce, soy sauce, vinegar, oil, hot sauce, garlic powder, cayenne, and three-quarters of the spring onions and toss until evenly coated.
3. Scrape the chicken and sauce into a metal cake pan and place the pan in the air fryer. Bake until the chicken is cooked through and the sauce is reduced to a thick glaze, about 20 minutes, flipping the chicken pieces halfway through.
4. Remove the pan from the air fryer. Spoon the chicken and sauce over rice and top with the remaining spring onions. Serve immediately.

CHAPTER 5

Fish and Seafood

Tandoori-Spiced Salmon and Potatoes ··· 30

Air Fryer Fish Sticks ·················· 30

Sole and Asparagus Bundles ············ 31

Roasted Salmon Fillets ················ 31

Orange-Mustard Glazed Salmon ········ 32

Crab Cakes with Lettuce and Apple Salad ·· 32

Bacon-Wrapped Scallops ··············· 33

Confetti Salmon Burgers ··············· 33

Crunchy Air Fried Cod Fillets ··········· 34

Thai Prawn Skewers with Peanut Dipping Sauce·· 34

Moroccan Spiced Halibut with Chickpea Salad ·· 35

Pecan-Crusted Tilapia ················· 35

Swordfish Skewers with Caponata ········ 36

Simple Salmon Bites ··················· 36

Roasted Cod with Lemon-Garlic Potatoes · 37

Vegetable and Fish Tacos ··············· 37

Tandoori-Spiced Salmon and Potatoes

SERVES 2

| **PREP TIME:** 10 minutes
| **COOK TIME:** 28 minutes

454 g fingerling potatoes
2 tbsps. vegetable oil, divided
Salt and freshly ground black pepper, to taste
1 tsp. ground turmeric
1 tsp. ground cumin
1 tsp. ground ginger
½ tsp. smoked paprika
¼ tsp. cayenne pepper
2 (170-g) skin-on salmon fillets

1. Preheat the air fryer to 190ºC.
2. In a bowl, toss the potatoes with 1 tbsp. of the oil until evenly coated. Season with salt and pepper. Transfer the potatoes to the air fryer and air fry for 20 minutes.
3. Meanwhile, in a bowl, combine the remaining 1 tbsp. oil, the turmeric, cumin, ginger, paprika, and cayenne. Add the salmon fillets and turn in the spice mixture until fully coated all over.
4. After the potatoes have cooked for 20 minutes, place the salmon fillets, skin-side up, on top of the potatoes, and continue cooking until the potatoes are tender, the salmon is cooked, and the salmon skin is slightly crisp.
5. Transfer the salmon fillets to two plates and serve with the potatoes while both are warm.

Air Fryer Fish Sticks

SERVES 4

| **PREP TIME:** 10 minutes
| **COOK TIME:** 10-12 minutes

Salt and pepper, to taste
680g skinless haddock fillets, 2-cm, sliced into 8-cm strips
250 g panko bread crumbs
1 tbsp. vegetable oil
30 g plain flour
60 g mayonnaise
2 large eggs
1 tbsp. Old Bay seasoning
Vegetable oil spray

1. Dissolve 75 g salt in 2 litres cold water in a large container. Add the haddock, cover, and let sit for 15 minutes.
2. Toss the panko with the oil in a bowl until evenly coated. Microwave, stirring frequently, until light golden brown, 2 to 4 minutes; transfer to a shallow dish. Whisk the flour, mayonnaise, eggs, Old Bay, ⅛ tsp. salt, and ⅛ tsp. pepper together in a second shallow dish.
3. Set a wire rack in a rimmed baking sheet and spray with vegetable oil spray. Remove the haddock from the brine and thoroughly pat dry with paper towels. Working with 1 piece at a time, dredge the haddock in the egg mixture, letting excess drip off, then coat with the panko mixture, pressing gently to adhere. Transfer the fish sticks to the prepared rack and freeze until firm, about 1 hour.
4. Preheat the air fryer to 205ºC. Lightly spray the air fryer basket with vegetable oil spray. Arrange up to 5 fish sticks in the prepared basket, spaced evenly apart. Air fry until fish sticks are golden and register 60ºC, 10 to 12 minutes, flipping and rotating fish sticks halfway through cooking.
5. Serve warm.

Sole and Asparagus Bundles

SERVES 2

| PREP TIME: 10 minutes
| COOK TIME: 14 minutes

227 g asparagus, trimmed
1 tsp. extra-virgin olive oil, divided
Salt and pepper, to taste
4 (85-g) skinless sole or flounder fillets, ¼ to ½ cm thick
4 tbsps. unsalted butter, softened
1 small shallot, minced
1 tbsp. chopped fresh tarragon
¼ tsp. lemon zest plus ½ tsp. juice
Vegetable oil spray

1. Preheat the air fryer to 150ºC.
2. Toss asparagus with ½ tsp. oil, pinch salt, and pinch pepper in a bowl. Cover and microwave until bright green and just tender, about 3 minutes, tossing halfway through microwaving. Uncover and set aside to cool slightly.
3. Make foil sling for air fryer basket by folding 1 long sheet of aluminum foil so it is 8-cm wide. Lay sheet of foil widthwise across basket, pressing foil into and up sides of basket. Fold excess foil as needed so that edges of foil are flush with top of basket. Lightly spray foil and basket with vegetable oil spray.
4. Pat sole dry with paper towels and season with salt and pepper. Arrange fillets skinned side up on cutting board, with thicker ends closest to you. Arrange asparagus evenly across base of each fillet, then tightly roll fillets away from you around asparagus to form tidy bundles.
5. Rub bundles evenly with remaining ½ tsp. oil and arrange seam side down on sling in prepared basket. Bake until asparagus is tender and sole flakes apart when gently prodded with a paring knife, 14 to 18 minutes, using a sling to rotate bundles halfway through cooking.
6. Combine butter, shallot, tarragon, and lemon zest and juice in a bowl. Using sling, carefully remove sole bundles from air fryer and transfer to individual plates. Top evenly with butter mixture and serve.

Roasted Salmon Fillets

SERVES 2

| PREP TIME: 5 minutes
| COOK TIME: 10 minutes

2 (227-g) skin-on salmon fillets, 3-cm thick
1 tsp. vegetable oil
Salt and pepper, to taste
Vegetable oil spray

1. Preheat the air fryer to 200ºC.
2. Make foil sling for air fryer basket by folding 1 long sheet of aluminum foil so it is 8-cm wide. Lay sheet of foil widthwise across basket, pressing foil into and up sides of basket. Fold excess foil as needed so that edges of foil are flush with top of basket. Lightly spray foil and basket with vegetable oil spray.
3. Pat salmon dry with paper towels, rub with oil, and season with salt and pepper. Arrange fillets skin side down on sling in prepared basket, spaced evenly apart. Air fry salmon until centre is still translucent when checked with the tip of a paring knife and registers 52ºC (for medium-rare), 10 to 14 minutes, using sling to rotate fillets halfway through cooking.
4. Using the sling, carefully remove salmon from air fryer. Slide fish spatula along underside of fillets and transfer to individual serving plates, leaving skin behind. Serve.

CHAPTER 5
Fish and Seafood

Orange-Mustard Glazed Salmon

SERVES 2

PREP TIME: 10 minutes
COOK TIME: 10 minutes

1 tbsp. orange marmalade
¼ tsp. grated orange zest plus 1 tbsp. juice
2 tsps. whole-grain mustard
2 (227-g) skin-on salmon fillets 3-cm thick
Salt and pepper, to taste
Vegetable oil spray

1. Preheat the air fryer to 200ºC.
2. Make foil sling for air fryer basket by folding 1 long sheet of aluminum foil so it is 8-cm wide. Lay sheet of foil widthwise across basket, pressing foil into and up sides of basket. Fold excess foil as needed so that edges of foil are flush with top of basket. Lightly spray foil and basket with vegetable oil spray.
3. Combine marmalade, orange zest and juice, and mustard in bowl. Pat salmon dry with paper towels and season with salt and pepper. Brush tops and sides of fillets evenly with glaze. Arrange fillets skin side down on sling in prepared basket, spaced evenly apart. Air fry salmon until centre is still translucent when checked with the tip of a paring knife and registers 55ºC (for medium-rare), 10 to 14 minutes, using sling to rotate fillets halfway through cooking.
4. Using the sling, carefully remove salmon from air fryer. Slide fish spatula along underside of fillets and transfer to individual serving plates, leaving skin behind. Serve.

Crab Cakes with Lettuce and Apple Salad

SERVES 2

PREP TIME: 10 minutes
COOK TIME: 13 minutes

227 g lump crab meat, picked over for shells
2 tbsps. panko bread crumbs
1 spring onion, minced
1 large egg
1 tbsp. mayonnaise
1½ tsps. Dijon mustard
Pinch of cayenne pepper
2 shallots, sliced thin
1 tbsp. extra-virgin olive oil, divided
1 tsp. lemon juice, plus lemon wedges for serving
⅛ tsp. salt
Pinch of pepper
½ (85-g) small head Bibb lettuce, torn into bite-size pieces
½ apple, cored and sliced thin

1. Preheat the air fryer to 200ºC.
2. Line large plate with triple layer of paper towels. Transfer crab meat to prepared plate and pat dry with additional paper towels. Combine panko, spring onion, egg, mayonnaise, mustard, and cayenne in a bowl. Using a rubber spatula, gently fold in crab meat until combined; discard paper towels. Divide crab mixture into 4 tightly packed balls, then flatten each into 2-cm-thick cake (cakes will be delicate). Transfer cakes to plate and refrigerate until firm, about 10 minutes.
3. Toss shallots with ½ tsp. oil in separate bowl; transfer to air fryer basket. Air fry until shallots are browned, 5 to 7 minutes, tossing once halfway through cooking. Return shallots to now-empty bowl and set aside.
4. Arrange crab cakes in air fryer basket, spaced evenly apart. Return basket to air fryer and air fry until crab cakes are light golden brown on both sides, 8 to 10 minutes, flipping and rotating cakes halfway through cooking.
5. Meanwhile, whisk remaining 2½ tsps. oil, lemon juice, salt, and pepper together in large bowl. Add lettuce, apple, and shallots and toss to coat. Serve crab cakes with salad, passing lemon wedges separately.

CHAPTER 5
Fish and Seafood

Bacon-Wrapped Scallops

SERVES 4

PREP TIME: 10 minutes
COOK TIME: 12 minutes

12 slices bacon
24 large sea scallops, tendons removed
1 tsp. plus 2 tbsps. extra-virgin olive oil, divided
Salt and pepper, to taste
6 (12-cm) wooden skewers
1 tbsp. cider vinegar
1 tsp. Dijon mustard
142 g baby spinach
1 fennel bulb, stalks discarded, bulb halved, cored, and sliced thin
142 g raspberries

1. Preheat the air fryer to 180ºC.
2. Line large plate with 4 layers of paper towels and arrange 6 slices bacon over towels in a single layer. Top with 4 more layers of paper towels and remaining 6 slices bacon. Cover with 2 layers of paper towels, place a second large plate on top, and press gently to flatten. Microwave until fat begins to render but bacon is still pliable, about 5 minutes.
3. Pat scallops dry with paper towels and toss with 1 tsp. oil, ⅛ tsp. salt, and ⅛ tsp. pepper in a bowl until evenly coated. Arrange 2 scallops side to side, flat side down, on the cutting board. Starting at narrow end, wrap 1 slice bacon tightly around sides of scallop bundle. (Bacon should overlap slightly; trim excess as needed.) Thread scallop bundle onto skewer through bacon. Repeat with remaining scallops and bacon, threading 2 bundles onto each skewer.
4. Arrange 3 skewers in air fryer basket, parallel to each other and spaced evenly apart. Arrange remaining 3 skewers on top, perpendicular to the bottom layer. Bake until bacon is crisp and scallops are firm and centres are opaque, 12 to 16 minutes, flipping and rotating skewers halfway through cooking.
5. Meanwhile, whisk remaining 2 tbsps. oil, vinegar, mustard, ⅛ tsp. salt, and ⅛ tsp. pepper in large serving bowl until combined. Add spinach, fennel, and raspberries and gently toss to coat. Serve skewers with salad.

Confetti Salmon Burgers

SERVES 4

PREP TIME: 10 minutes
COOK TIME: 12 minutes

397 g cooked fresh or canned salmon, flaked with a fork
15 g minced spring onion, white and light green parts only
25 g minced red pepper
25 g minced celery
2 small lemons
1 tsp. crab boil seasoning such as Old Bay
½ tsp. salt
½ tsp. black pepper
1 egg, beaten
62 g fresh bread crumbs
Vegetable oil, for spraying

1. In a large bowl, combine the salmon, vegetables, the zest and juice of 1 of the lemons, crab boil seasoning, salt, and pepper. Add the egg and bread crumbs and stir to combine. Form the mixture into 4 patties weighing approximately 142 g each. Chill until firm, about 15 minutes.
2. Preheat the air fryer to 200ºC.
3. Spray the salmon patties with oil on all sides and spray the air fryer basket to prevent sticking. Air fry for 12 minutes, flipping halfway through, until the burgers are browned and cooked through. Cut the remaining lemon into 4 wedges and serve with the burgers. Serve immediately.

Crunchy Air Fried Cod Fillets

SERVES 2

| PREP TIME: 10 minutes
| COOK TIME: 12 minutes

40 g panko bread crumbs
1 tsp. vegetable oil
1 small shallot, minced
1 small garlic clove, minced
½ tsp. minced fresh thyme
Salt and pepper, to taste
1 tbsp. minced fresh parsley
1 tbsp. mayonnaise
1 large egg yolk
¼ tsp. grated lemon zest, plus lemon wedges for serving
2 (227-g) skinless cod fillets, 2 1/2 -cm thick
Vegetable oil spray

1. Preheat the air fryer to 150°C.
2. Make foil sling for air fryer basket by folding 1 long sheet of aluminum foil so it is 8-cm wide. Lay sheet of foil widthwise across basket, pressing foil into and up sides of basket. Fold excess foil as needed so that edges of foil are flush with top of basket. Lightly spray the foil and basket with vegetable oil spray.
3. Toss the panko with the oil in a bowl until evenly coated. Stir in the shallot, garlic, thyme, ¼ tsp. salt, and ⅛ tsp. pepper. Microwave, stirring frequently, until the panko is light golden brown, about 2 minutes. Transfer to a shallow dish and let cool slightly; stir in the parsley. Whisk the mayonnaise, egg yolk, lemon zest, and ⅛ tsp. pepper together in another bowl.
4. Pat the cod dry with paper towels and season with salt and pepper. Arrange the fillets, skinned-side down, on plate and brush tops evenly with mayonnaise mixture. (Tuck thinner tail ends of fillets under themselves as needed to create uniform pieces.) Working with 1 fillet at a time, dredge the coated side in panko mixture, pressing gently to adhere. Arrange the fillets, crumb-side up, on sling in the prepared basket, spaced evenly apart.
5. Bake for 12 to 16 minutes, using a sling to rotate fillets halfway through cooking. Using a sling, carefully remove cod from air fryer. Serve with the lemon wedges.

Thai Prawn Skewers with Peanut Dipping Sauce

SERVES 2

| PREP TIME: 15 minutes
| COOK TIME: 6 minutes

Salt and pepper, to taste
340 g extra-large prawn, peeled and deveined
1 tbsp. vegetable oil
1 tsp. honey
½ tsp. grated lime zest plus 1 tbsp. juice, plus lime wedges for serving
6 (12-cm) wooden skewers
3 tbsps. creamy peanut butter
3 tbsps. hot tap water
1 tbsp. chopped fresh coriander
1 tsp. fish sauce

1. Preheat the air fryer to 200°C.
2. Dissolve 2 tbsps. salt in 1 litre cold water in a large container. Add prawns, cover, and refrigerate for 15 minutes.
3. Remove prawns from brine and pat dry with paper towels. Whisk oil, honey, lime zest, and ¼ tsp. pepper together in a large bowl. Add prawns and toss to coat. Thread prawns onto skewers, leaving about ½-cm between each prawn (3 or 4 prawns per skewer).
4. Arrange 3 skewers in air fryer basket, parallel to each other and spaced evenly apart. Arrange remaining 3 skewers on top, perpendicular to the bottom layer. Air fry until prawns are opaque throughout, 6 to 8 minutes, flipping and rotating skewers halfway through cooking.
5. Whisk peanut butter, hot tap water, lime juice, coriander, and fish sauce together in a bowl until smooth. Serve skewers with peanut dipping sauce and lime wedges.

Moroccan Spiced Halibut with Chickpea Salad

SERVES 2

| PREP TIME: 15 minutes
| COOK TIME: 12 minutes

¾ tsp. ground coriander
½ tsp. ground cumin
¼ tsp. ground ginger
⅛ tsp. ground cinnamon
Salt and pepper, to taste
2 (227-g) skinless halibut fillets, 2 ½ cm thick
4 tsps. extra-virgin olive oil, divided, plus extra for drizzling
1 (425-g) can chickpeas, rinsed
1 tbsp. lemon juice, plus lemon wedges for serving
1 tsp. harissa
½ tsp. honey
2 carrots, peeled and shredded
2 tbsps. chopped fresh mint, divided
Vegetable oil spray

1. Preheat the air fryer to 150°C.
2. Make foil sling for air fryer basket by folding 1 long sheet of aluminum foil so it is 8-cm wide. Lay sheet of foil widthwise across basket, pressing foil into and up sides of basket. Fold excess foil as needed so that edges of foil are flush with top of basket. Lightly spray foil and basket with vegetable oil spray.
3. Combine coriander, cumin, ginger, cinnamon, ⅛ tsp. salt, and ⅛ tsp. pepper in a small bowl. Pat halibut dry with paper towels, rub with 1 tsp. oil, and sprinkle all over with spice mixture. Arrange fillets skinned side down on sling in prepared basket, spaced evenly apart. Bake until halibut flakes apart when gently prodded with a paring knife and registers 60°C, 12 to 16 minutes, using the sling to rotate fillets halfway through cooking.
4. Meanwhile, microwave chickpeas in medium bowl until heated through, about 2 minutes. Stir in remaining 1 tbsp. oil, lemon juice, harissa, honey, ⅛ tsp. salt, and ⅛ tsp. pepper. Add carrots and 1 tbsp. mint and toss to combine. Season with salt and pepper, to taste.
5. Using sling, carefully remove halibut from air fryer and transfer to individual plates. Sprinkle with remaining 1 tbsp. mint and drizzle with extra oil to taste. Serve with salad and lemon wedges.

Pecan-Crusted Tilapia

SERVES 4

| PREP TIME: 10 minutes
| COOK TIME: 10 minutes

190 g pecans
90 g panko bread crumbs
95 g plain flour
2 tbsps. Cajun seasoning
2 eggs, beaten with 2 tbsps. water
4 (170-g) tilapia fillets
Vegetable oil, for spraying
Lemon wedges, for serving

1. Grind the pecans in the food processor until they resemble coarse meal. Combine the ground pecans with the panko on a plate. On a second plate, combine the flour and Cajun seasoning. Dry the tilapia fillets using paper towels and dredge them in the flour mixture, shaking off any excess. Dip the fillets in the egg mixture and then dredge them in the pecan and panko mixture, pressing the coating onto the fillets. Place the breaded fillets on a plate or rack.
2. Preheat the air fryer to 190°C. Spray both sides of the breaded fillets with oil. Carefully transfer 2 of the fillets to the air fryer basket and air fry for 9 to 10 minutes, flipping once halfway through, until the flesh is opaque and flaky. Repeat with the remaining fillets.
3. Serve immediately with lemon wedges.

Swordfish Skewers with Caponata

SERVES 2

| PREP TIME: 15 minutes
| COOK TIME: 20 minutes

1 (283-g) small Italian aubergine, cut into 2-cm pieces
170 g cherry tomatoes
3 spring onions, cut into 4-cm long
2 tbsps. extra-virgin olive oil, divided
Salt and pepper, to taste
340 g skinless swordfish steaks, 2 ½ cm thick, cut into 2-cm pieces
2 tsps. honey, divided
2 tsps. ground coriander, divided
1 tsp. grated lemon zest, divided
1 tsp. juice
4 (12-cm) wooden skewers
1 garlic clove, minced
½ tsp. ground cumin
1 tbsp. chopped fresh basil

1. Preheat the air fryer to 205°C.
2. Toss aubergine, tomatoes, and spring onions with 1 tbsp. oil, ¼ tsp. salt, and ⅛ tsp. pepper in bowl; transfer to air fryer basket. Air fry until aubergine is softened and browned and tomatoes have begun to burst, about 14 minutes, tossing halfway through cooking. Transfer vegetables to cutting board and set aside to cool slightly.
3. Pat swordfish dry with paper towels. Combine 1 tsp. oil, 1 tsp. honey, 1 tsp. coriander, ½ tsp. lemon zest, ⅛ tsp. salt, and pinch pepper in a clean bowl. Add swordfish and toss to coat. Thread swordfish onto skewers, leaving about ½-cm between each piece (3 or 4 pieces per skewer).
4. Arrange skewers in air fryer basket, spaced evenly apart. (Skewers may overlap slightly.) Return basket to air fryer and air fry until swordfish is browned and registers 60°C, 6 to 8 minutes, flipping and rotating skewers halfway through cooking.
5. Meanwhile, combine remaining 2 tsps. oil, remaining 1 tsp. honey, remaining 1 tsp. coriander, remaining ½ tsp. lemon zest, lemon juice, garlic, cumin, ¼ tsp. salt, and ⅛ tsp. pepper in large bowl. Microwave, stirring once, until fragrant, about 30 seconds. Coarsely chop the cooked vegetables, transfer to bowl with dressing, along with any accumulated juices, and gently toss to combine. Stir in basil and season with salt and pepper to taste. Serve skewers with caponata.

Simple Salmon Bites

SERVES 4

| PREP TIME: 15 minutes
| COOK TIME: 10-15 minutes

4 (142-g) cans pink salmon, skinless, boneless in water, drained
2 eggs, beaten
125 g whole-wheat panko bread crumbs
4 tbsps. finely minced red pepper
2 tbsps. parsley flakes
2 tsps. Old Bay seasoning
Cooking spray

1. Preheat the air fryer to 180°C.
2. Spray the air fryer basket lightly with cooking spray.
3. In a medium bowl, mix the salmon, eggs, panko bread crumbs, red pepper, parsley flakes, and Old Bay seasoning.
4. Using a small cookie scoop, form the mixture into 20 balls.
5. Place the salmon bites in the air fryer basket in a single layer and spray lightly with cooking spray. You may need to cook them in batches.
6. Air fry until crispy for 10 to 15 minutes, shaking the basket a couple of times for even cooking.
7. Serve immediately.

Roasted Cod with Lemon-Garlic Potatoes

SERVES 2

PREP TIME: 10 minutes **COOK TIME:** 28 minutes	3 tbsps. unsalted butter, softened, divided 2 garlic cloves, minced 1 lemon, grated to yield 2 tsps. zest and sliced ½ cm thick Salt and pepper, to taste 1 large russet potato (340-g), unpeeled, sliced ½ cm thick 1 tbsp. minced fresh parsley, chives, or tarragon 2 (227-g) skinless cod fillets, 2 ½ cm thick Vegetable oil spray

1. Preheat the air fryer to 200°C.
2. Make foil sling for air fryer basket by folding 1 long sheet of aluminum foil so it is 8-cm wide. Lay sheet of foil widthwise across basket, pressing foil into and up sides of basket. Fold excess foil as needed so that edges of foil are flush with top of basket. Lightly spray the foil and basket with vegetable oil spray.
3. Microwave 1 tbsp. butter, garlic, 1 tsp. lemon zest, ¼ tsp. salt, and ⅛ tsp. pepper in a medium bowl, stirring once, until the butter is melted and the mixture is fragrant, about 30 seconds. Add the potato slices and toss to coat. Shingle the potato slices on sling in prepared basket to create 2 even layers. Air fry until potato slices are spotty brown and just tender, 16 to 18 minutes, using a sling to rotate potatoes halfway through cooking.
4. Combine the remaining 2 tbsps. butter, remaining 1 tsp. lemon zest, and parsley in a small bowl. Pat the cod dry with paper towels and season with salt and pepper. Place the fillets, skinned-side down, on top of potato slices, spaced evenly apart. (Tuck thinner tail ends of fillets under themselves as needed to create uniform pieces.) Dot the fillets with the butter mixture and top with the lemon slices. Return the basket to the air fryer and air fry until the cod flakes apart when gently prodded with a paring knife and registers 60°C, 12 to 15 minutes, using a sling to rotate the potato slices and cod halfway through cooking.
5. Using a sling, carefully remove potatoes and cod from air fryer. Cut the potato slices into 2 portions between fillets using fish spatula. Slide spatula along underside of potato slices and transfer with cod to individual plates. Serve.

Vegetable and Fish Tacos

SERVES 4

PREP TIME: 10 minutes **COOK TIME:** 9-12 minutes	454 g white fish fillets 2 tsps. olive oil 3 tbsps. freshly squeezed lemon juice, divided 30 g chopped red cabbage 1 large carrot, grated 125 g low-sodium salsa 90 g low-fat Greek yogurt 4 soft low-sodium whole-wheat tortillas

1. Preheat the air fryer to 200°C.
2. Brush the fish with the olive oil and sprinkle with 1 tbsp. of lemon juice. Air fry in the air fryer basket for 9 to 12 minutes, or until the fish just flakes when tested with a fork.
3. Meanwhile, in a medium bowl, stir together the remaining 2 tbsps. of lemon juice, the red cabbage, carrot, salsa, and yogurt.
4. When the fish is cooked, remove it from the air fryer basket and break it up into large pieces.
5. Offer the fish, tortillas, and the cabbage mixture, and let each person assemble a taco.
6. Serve immediately.

CHAPTER 6
Meats

Simple Pulled Pork 39

Barbecue Pork Ribs 39

Char Siew 40

Rosemary Ribeye Steaks 40

Easy Beef Schnitzel 41

Swedish Beef Meatballs 41

Teriyaki Pork and Mushroom Rolls 42

Vietnamese Pork Chops 42

Provolone Stuffed Beef and Pork Meatballs 43

Classic Spring Rolls 43

Smoked Beef 43

Ritzy Skirt Steak Fajitas 44

Beef and Vegetable Cubes 44

Beef Steak Fingers 45

Hearty Sweet and Sour Pork 45

Simple Pulled Pork

SERVES 1

| PREP TIME: 5 minutes
| COOK TIME: 24 minutes

2 tbsps. barbecue dry rub
454 g pork tenderloin
80 g heavy cream
1 tsp. butter

1. Preheat the air fryer to 190ºC.
2. Massage the dry rub into the tenderloin, coating it well.
3. Air fry the tenderloin in the air fryer for 20 minutes. When air fried, shred with two forks.
4. Add the heavy cream and butter into the air fryer along with the shredded pork and stir well. Air fry for a further 4 minutes.
5. Allow to cool, then serve.

Barbecue Pork Ribs

SERVES 4

| PREP TIME: 5 minutes
| COOK TIME: 30 minutes

1 tbsp. barbecue dry rub
1 tsp. mustard
1 tbsp. apple cider vinegar
1 tsp. sesame oil
454 g pork ribs, chopped

1. Combine the dry rub, mustard, apple cider vinegar, and sesame oil, then coat the ribs with this mixture. Refrigerate the ribs for 20 minutes.
2. Preheat the air fryer to 180ºC.
3. When the ribs are ready, place them in the air fryer and air fry for 15 minutes. Flip them and air fry on the other side for a further 15 minutes.
4. Serve immediately.

CHAPTER 6
Meats

Char Siew

SERVES 4-6

| **PREP TIME:** 10 minutes
| **COOK TIME:** 20 minutes

1 strip of pork shoulder with a good amount of fat marbling
Olive oil, for brushing the pan
Marinade:
1 tsp. sesame oil
4 tbsps. raw honey
1 tsp. low-sodium dark soy sauce
1 tsp. light soy sauce
1 tbsp. rose wine
2 tbsps. Hoisin sauce

1. Combine all the marinade ingredients together in a Ziploc bag. Put pork in bag, making sure all sections of pork strip are engulfed in the marinade. Chill for 3 to 24 hours.
2. Take out the strip 30 minutes before planning to roast and preheat the air fryer to 180ºC.
3. Put foil on small pan and brush with olive oil. Put marinated pork strip onto prepared pan.
4. Roast in the preheated air fryer for 20 minutes.
5. Glaze with marinade every 5 to 10 minutes.
6. Remove strip and leave to cool a few minutes before slicing.
7. Serve immediately.

Rosemary Ribeye Steaks

SERVES 2

| **PREP TIME:** 10 minutes
| **COOK TIME:** 15 minutes

56 g butter
1 clove garlic, minced
Salt and ground black pepper, to taste
1½ tbsps. balsamic vinegar
15 g rosemary, chopped
2 ribeye steaks

1. Melt the butter in a skillet over medium heat. Add the garlic and fry until fragrant.
2. Remove the skillet from the heat and add the salt, pepper, and vinegar. Allow it to cool.
3. Add the rosemary, then pour the mixture into a Ziploc bag.
4. Put the ribeye steaks in the bag and shake well, coating the meat well. Refrigerate for an hour, then allow to sit for a further twenty minutes.
5. Preheat the air fryer to 200ºC and set the rack inside. Air fry the ribeyes for 15 minutes.
6. Take care when removing the steaks from the air fryer and plate up.
7. Serve immediately.

CHAPTER 6
Meats

Easy Beef Schnitzel

SERVES 1

| **PREP TIME:** 5 minutes
| **COOK TIME:** 12 minutes

60 g friendly bread crumbs
2 tbsps. olive oil
Pepper and salt, to taste
1 egg, beaten
1 thin beef schnitzel

1. Preheat the air fryer to 180ºC.
2. In a shallow dish, combine the bread crumbs, oil, pepper, and salt.
3. In a second shallow dish, place the beaten egg.
4. Dredge the schnitzel in the egg before rolling it in the bread crumbs.
5. Put the coated schnitzel in the air fryer basket and air fry for 12 minutes. Flip the schnitzel halfway through.
6. Serve immediately.

Swedish Beef Meatballs

SERVES 8

| **PREP TIME:** 10 minutes
| **COOK TIME:** 12 minutes

454 g beef mince
1 egg, beaten
2 carrots, shredded
2 bread slices, crumbled
1 small onion, minced
½ tsps. garlic salt
Pepper and salt, to taste
225 g tomato sauce
450 g pasta sauce

1. Preheat the air fryer to 200ºC.
2. In a bowl, combine the beef mince, egg, carrots, crumbled bread, onion, garlic salt, pepper and salt.
3. Divide the mixture into equal amounts and shape each one into a small meatball.
4. Put them in the air fryer basket and air fry for 7 minutes.
5. Transfer the meatballs to an oven-safe dish and top with the tomato sauce and pasta sauce.
6. Set the dish into the air fryer basket and allow to air fry at 160ºC for 5 more minutes. Serve hot.

CHAPTER 6
Meats

Teriyaki Pork and Mushroom Rolls

SERVES 6

| **PREP TIME:** 10 minutes
| **COOK TIME:** 8 minutes

4 tbsps. brown sugar
4 tbsps. mirin
4 tbsps. soy sauce
1 tsp. almond flour
4-cm ginger, chopped
6 (113-g) pork belly slices
170 g Enoki mushrooms

1. Mix the brown sugar, mirin, soy sauce, almond flour, and ginger together until brown sugar dissolves.
2. Take pork belly slices and wrap around a bundle of mushrooms. Brush each roll with teriyaki sauce. Chill for half an hour.
3. Preheat the air fryer to 180ºC and add marinated pork rolls.
4. Air fry for 8 minutes. Flip the rolls halfway through.
5. Serve immediately.

Vietnamese Pork Chops

SERVES 2

| **PREP TIME:** 15 minutes
| **COOK TIME:** 12 minutes

1 tbsp. chopped shallot
1 tbsp. chopped garlic
1 tbsp. fish sauce
3 tbsps. lemongrass
1 tsp. soy sauce
1 tbsp. brown sugar
1 tbsp. olive oil
1 tsp. ground black pepper
2 pork chops

1. Combine shallot, garlic, fish sauce, lemongrass, soy sauce, brown sugar, olive oil, and pepper in a bowl. Stir to mix well.
2. Put the pork chops in the bowl. Toss to coat well. Place the bowl in the refrigerator to marinate for 2 hours.
3. Preheat the air fryer to 200ºC.
4. Remove the pork chops from the bowl and discard the marinade. Transfer the chops into the air fryer.
5. Air fry for 12 minutes or until lightly browned. Flip the pork chops halfway through the cooking time.
6. Remove the pork chops from the basket and serve hot.

CHAPTER 6
Meats

Provolone Stuffed Beef and Pork Meatballs

SERVES 4-6

| PREP TIME: 15 minutes
| COOK TIME: 12 minutes

1 tbsp. olive oil
1 small onion, finely chopped
1 to 2 cloves garlic, minced
340 g beef mince
340 g pork mince
90 g bread crumbs
22 g grated Parmesan cheese
15 g finely chopped fresh parsley
½ tsp. dried oregano
1½ tsps. salt
Freshly ground black pepper, to taste
2 eggs, lightly beaten
142 g sharp or aged provolone cheese, cut into 2-cm cubes

1. Preheat a skillet over medium-high heat. Add the oil and cook the onion and garlic until tender, but not browned.
2. Transfer the onion and garlic to a large bowl and add the beef, pork, bread crumbs, Parmesan cheese, parsley, oregano, salt, pepper and eggs. Mix well until all the ingredients are combined. Divide the mixture into 12 evenly sized balls. Make one meatball at a time, by pressing a hole in the meatball mixture with the finger and pushing a piece of provolone cheese into the hole. Mold the meat back into a ball, enclosing the cheese.
3. Preheat the air fryer to 190ºC.
4. Working in two batches, transfer six of the meatballs to the air fryer basket and air fry for 12 minutes, shaking the basket and turning the meatballs twice during the cooking process. Repeat with the remaining 6 meatballs. Serve warm.

Classic Spring Rolls

SERVES 20

| PREP TIME: 10 minutes
| COOK TIME: 8 minutes

25 g noodles
227 g beef mince
1 tsp. soy sauce
130 g fresh mix vegetables
3 garlic cloves, minced
1 small onion, diced
1 tbsp. sesame oil
1 packet spring roll sheets
2 tbsps. cold water

1. Cook the noodle in enough hot water to soften them up, drain them and snip them to make them shorter.
2. In a frying pan over medium heat, cook the beef, soy sauce, mixed vegetables, garlic, and onion in sesame oil until the beef is cooked through. Take the pan off the heat and throw in the noodles. Mix well to incorporate everything.
3. Unroll a spring roll sheet and lay it flat. Scatter the filling diagonally across it and roll it up, brushing the edges lightly with water to act as an adhesive. Repeat until you have used up all the sheets and the filling.
4. Preheat the air fryer to 180ºC.
5. Coat each spring roll with a light brushing of oil and transfer to the air fryer.
6. Air fry for 8 minutes and serve hot.

Smoked Beef

SERVES 8

| PREP TIME: 10 minutes
| COOK TIME: 45 minutes

907 g roast beef, at room temperature
2 tbsps. extra-virgin olive oil
1 tsp. sea salt flakes
1 tsp. ground black pepper
1 tsp. smoked paprika
Few dashes of liquid smoke
2 jalapeño peppers, thinly sliced

1. Preheat the air fryer to 165ºC.
2. With kitchen towels, pat the beef dry.
3. Massage the extra-virgin olive oil, salt, black pepper, and paprika into the meat. Cover with liquid smoke.
4. Put the beef in the air fryer and roast for 30 minutes. Flip the roast over and allow to roast for another 15 minutes.
5. When cooked through, serve topped with sliced jalapeños.

Ritzy Skirt Steak Fajitas

SERVES 4

| PREP TIME: 15 minutes
| COOK TIME: 30 minutes

- 2 tbsps. olive oil
- 60 ml lime juice
- 1 clove garlic, minced
- ½ tsp. ground cumin
- ½ tsp. hot sauce
- ½ tsp. salt
- 2 tbsps. chopped fresh coriander
- 454 g skirt steak
- 1 onion, sliced
- 1 tsp. chili powder
- 1 red pepper, sliced
- 1 green pepper, sliced
- Salt and freshly ground black pepper, to taste
- 8 flour tortillas
- Toppings:
- Shredded lettuce
- Crumbled Queso Fresco (or grated Cheddar cheese)
- Sliced black olives
- Diced tomatoes
- Sour cream
- Guacamole

1. Combine the olive oil, lime juice, garlic, cumin, hot sauce, salt and coriander in a shallow dish. Add the skirt steak and turn it over several times to coat all sides. Pierce the steak with a needle-style meat tenderizer or paring knife. Marinate the steak in the refrigerator for at least 3 hours, or overnight. When you are ready to cook, remove the steak from the refrigerator and let it sit at room temperature for 30 minutes.
2. Preheat the air fryer to 200ºC.
3. Toss the onion slices with the chili powder and a little olive oil and transfer them to the air fryer basket. Air fry for 5 minutes. Add the red and green peppers to the air fryer basket with the onions, season with salt and pepper and air fry for 8 more minutes, until the onions and peppers are soft. Transfer the vegetables to a dish and cover with aluminum foil to keep warm.
4. Put the skirt steak in the air fryer basket and pour the marinade over the top. Air fry at 200ºC for 12 minutes. Flip the steak over and air fry for an additional 5 minutes. Transfer the cooked steak to a cutting board and let the steak rest for a few minutes. If the peppers and onions need to be heated, return them to the air fryer for just 1 to 2 minutes.
5. Thinly slice the steak at an angle, cutting against the grain of the steak. Serve the steak with the onions and peppers, the warm tortillas and the fajita toppings on the side.
6. Serve immediately.

Beef and Vegetable Cubes

SERVES 4

| PREP TIME: 15 minutes
| COOK TIME: 17 minutes

- 2 tbsps. olive oil
- 1 tbsp. apple cider vinegar
- 1 tsp. fine sea salt
- ½ tsps. ground black pepper
- 1 tsp. shallot powder
- ¾ tsp. smoked cayenne pepper
- ½ tsps. garlic powder
- ¼ tsp. ground cumin
- 454 g top round steak, cut into cubes
- 113 g broccoli, cut into florets
- 113 g mushrooms, sliced
- 1 tsp. dried basil
- 1 tsp. celery seeds

1. Massage the olive oil, vinegar, salt, black pepper, shallot powder, cayenne pepper, garlic powder, and cumin into the cubed steak, ensuring to coat each piece evenly.
2. Allow to marinate for a minimum of 3 hours.
3. Preheat the air fryer to 185ºC.
4. Put the beef cubes in the air fryer basket and air fry for 12 minutes.
5. When the steak is cooked through, place it in a bowl.
6. Wipe the grease from the basket and pour in the vegetables. Season them with basil and celery seeds.
7. Increase the temperature of the air fryer to 200ºC and air fry for 5 to 6 minutes. When the vegetables are hot, serve them with the steak.

Beef Steak Fingers

SERVES 4

PREP TIME: 5 minutes **COOK TIME:** 8 minutes	4 small beef cube steaks Salt and ground black pepper, to taste 62 g flour Cooking spray

1. Preheat the air fryer to 200ºC.
2. Cut cube steaks into 2-cm wide strips.
3. Sprinkle lightly with salt and pepper to taste.
4. Roll in flour to coat all sides.
5. Spritz air fryer basket with cooking spray.
6. Put steak strips in air fryer basket in a single layer. Spritz top of steak strips with cooking spray.
7. Air fry for 4 minutes, turn strips over, and spritz with cooking spray.
8. Air fry 4 more minutes and test with fork for doneness. Steak fingers should be crispy outside with no red juices inside.
9. Repeat steps 6 through 8 to air fry remaining strips.
10. Serve immediately.

Hearty Sweet and Sour Pork

SERVES 2-4

PREP TIME: 20 minutes **COOK TIME:** 14 minutes	37 g plain flour 35 g cornflour 2 tsps. Chinese five-spice powder 1 tsp. salt Freshly ground black pepper, to taste 1 egg 2 tbsps. milk 340 g boneless pork, cut into 2-cm cubes Vegetable or rapeseed oil 150 g large chunks of red and green peppers 117 g ketchup 2 tbsps. rice wine vinegar or apple cider vinegar 2 tbsps. brown sugar 60 ml orange juice 1 tbsp. soy sauce 1 clove garlic, minced 200 g cubed pineapple Chopped spring onions, for garnish

1. Set up a dredging station with two bowls. Combine the flour, cornflour, Chinese five-spice powder, salt and pepper in one large bowl. Whisk the egg and milk together in a second bowl. Dredge the pork cubes in the flour mixture first, then dip them into the egg and then back into the flour to coat on all sides. Spray the coated pork cubes with vegetable or rapeseed oil.
2. Preheat the air fryer to 200ºC.
3. Toss the pepper chunks with a little oil and air fry for 5 minutes, shaking the basket halfway through the cooking time.
4. While the peppers are cooking, start making the sauce. Combine the ketchup, rice wine vinegar, brown sugar, orange juice, soy sauce, and garlic in a medium saucepan and bring the mixture to a boil on the stovetop. Reduce the heat and simmer for 5 minutes. When the peppers have finished air frying, add them to the saucepan along with the pineapple chunks. Simmer the peppers and pineapple in the sauce for an additional 2 minutes. Set aside and keep warm.
5. Add the dredged pork cubes to the air fryer basket and air fry at 205ºC for 6 minutes, shaking the basket to turn the cubes over for the last minute of the cooking process.
6. When ready to serve, toss the cooked pork with the pineapple, peppers and sauce. Serve garnished with chopped spring onions.

CHAPTER 7
Wraps and Sandwiches

Nugget and Veggie Taco Wraps 47

Tuna and Lettuce Wraps 47

Cheesy Prawn Sandwich 48

Chicken Pita Sandwich 48

Veggie Salsa Wraps 49

Lettuce Fajita Meatball Wraps 49

Tuna Muffin Sandwich 49

Nugget and Veggie Taco Wraps

SERVES 4

PREP TIME: 5 minutes
COOK TIME: 15 minutes

1 tbsp. water
4 pieces commercial vegan nuggets, chopped
1 small yellow onion, diced
1 small red pepper, chopped
2 cobs grilled corn kernels
4 large corn tortillas
Mixed greens, for garnish

1. Preheat the air fryer to 200ºC.
2. Over a medium heat, sauté the nuggets in the water with the onion, corn kernels and pepper in a skillet, then remove from the heat.
3. Fill the tortillas with the nuggets and vegetables and fold them up. Transfer to the inside of the fryer and air fry for 15 minutes.
4. Once crispy, serve immediately, garnished with the mixed greens.

Tuna and Lettuce Wraps

SERVES 4

PREP TIME: 10 minutes
COOK TIME: 4-7 minutes

454 g fresh tuna steak, cut into 2-cm cubes
1 tbsp. grated fresh ginger
2 garlic cloves, minced
½ tsp. toasted sesame oil
4 low-sodium whole-wheat tortillas
60 g low-fat mayonnaise
30 g shredded romaine lettuce
1 red pepper, thinly sliced

1. Preheat the air fryer to 200ºC.
2. In a medium bowl, mix the tuna, ginger, garlic, and sesame oil. Let it stand for 10 minutes.
3. Air fry the tuna in the air fryer basket for 4 to 7 minutes, or until lightly browned.
4. Make the wraps with the tuna, tortillas, mayonnaise, lettuce, and pepper.
5. Serve immediately.

Cheesy Prawn Sandwich

SERVES 4

| **PREP TIME:** 10 minutes
| **COOK TIME:** 5-7 minutes

290 g shredded Colby, Cheddar, or Havarti cheese
1 (170-g) can tiny prawns, drained
3 tbsps. mayonnaise
2 tbsps. minced spring onion
4 slices whole grain or whole-wheat bread
2 tbsps. softened butter

1. Preheat the air fryer to 205ºC.
2. In a medium bowl, combine the cheese, prawn, mayonnaise, and spring onion, and mix well.
3. Spread this mixture on two of the slices of bread. Top with the other slices of bread to make two sandwiches. Spread the sandwiches lightly with butter.
4. Air fry for 5 to 7 minutes, or until the bread is browned and crisp and the cheese is melted.
5. Cut in half and serve warm.

Chicken Pita Sandwich

SERVES 4

| **PREP TIME:** 10 minutes
| **COOK TIME:** 9-11 minutes

2 boneless, skinless chicken breasts, cut into 2-cm cubes
1 small red onion, sliced
1 red pepper, sliced
80 ml Italian salad dressing, divided
½ tsp. dried thyme
4 pita pockets, split
55 g torn butter lettuce
200 g chopped cherry tomatoes

1. Preheat the air fryer to 190ºC.
2. Place the chicken, onion, and pepper in the air fryer basket. Drizzle with 1 tbsp. of the Italian salad dressing, add the thyme, and toss.
3. Bake for 9 to 11 minutes, or until the chicken is 75ºC on a food thermometer, stirring once during cooking time.
4. Transfer the chicken and vegetables to a bowl and toss with the remaining salad dressing.
5. Assemble sandwiches with the pita pockets, butter lettuce, and cherry tomatoes. Serve immediately.

CHAPTER 7
Wraps and Sandwiches

Veggie Salsa Wraps

SERVES 4

| PREP TIME: 5 minutes
| COOK TIME: 7 minutes

50 g red onion, sliced
1 courgette, chopped
1 poblano pepper, deseeded and finely chopped
1 head lettuce
130 g salsa
227 g Mozzarella cheese

1. Preheat the air fryer to 200ºC.
2. Place the red onion, courgette, and poblano pepper in the air fryer basket and air fry for 7 minutes, or until they are tender and fragrant.
3. Divide the veggie mixture among the lettuce leaves and spoon the salsa over the top. Finish off with Mozzarella cheese. Wrap the lettuce leaves around the filling.
4. Serve immediately.

Lettuce Fajita Meatball Wraps

SERVES 4

| PREP TIME: 10 minutes
| COOK TIME: 10 minutes

454 g 85% lean beef mince
130 g salsa, plus more for serving
15 g chopped onions
20 g diced green or red peppers
1 large egg, beaten
1 tsp. fine sea salt
½ tsp. chili powder
½ tsp. ground cumin
1 clove garlic, minced
Cooking spray
For Serving:
8 leaves Boston lettuce
Pico de gallo or salsa
Lime slices

1. Preheat the air fryer to 180ºC. Spray the air fryer basket with cooking spray.
2. In a large bowl, mix together all the ingredients until well combined.
3. Shape the meat mixture into eight 2-cm balls. Place the meatballs in the air fryer basket, leaving a little space between them. Air fry for 10 minutes, or until cooked through and no longer pink inside and the internal temperature reaches 63ºC.
4. Serve each meatball on a lettuce leaf, topped with pico de gallo or salsa. Serve with lime slices.

Tuna Muffin Sandwich

SERVES 4

| PREP TIME: 8 minutes
| COOK TIME: 4-8 minutes

1 (170-g) can chunk light tuna, drained
55 g mayonnaise
2 tbsps. mustard
1 tbsp. lemon juice
2 spring onions, minced
3 English muffins, split with a fork
3 tbsps. softened butter
6 thin slices Provolone or Muenster cheese

1. Preheat the air fryer to 200ºC.
2. In a small bowl, combine the tuna, mayonnaise, mustard, lemon juice, and spring onions. Set aside.
3. Butter the cut side of the English muffins. Bake, butter-side up, in the air fryer for 2 to 4 minutes, or until light golden brown. Remove the muffins from the air fryer basket.
4. Top each muffin with one slice of cheese and return to the air fryer. Bake for 2 to 4 minutes or until the cheese melts and starts to brown.
5. Remove the muffins from the air fryer, top with the tuna mixture, and serve.

CHAPTER 8

Snacks and Desserts

Spicy Chicken Wings ················ 51

Lemony Chicken Drumsticks ················ 51

Coconut-Crusted Prawns ················ 52

BBQ Pork Ribs ················ 52

Spiced Sweet Potato Fries ················ 53

Spiced Mixed Nuts ················ 53

Crispy Apple Chips ················ 54

Simple Apple Turnovers ················ 54

Spice Cookies ················ 55

Pineapple Galette ················ 55

Rosemary-Garlic Shoestring Fries ················ 56

Crispy Spiced Chickpeas ················ 56

Bacon-Wrapped Prawns and Jalapeño ··· 56

Baked Ricotta ················ 57

Lemony Apple Butter ················ 57

Spicy Chicken Wings

SERVES 2-4

| **PREP TIME:** 5 minutes
| **COOK TIME:** 20 minutes

567 g chicken wings, separated into flats and drumsticks
1 tsp. baking powder
1 tsp. cayenne pepper
¼ tsp. garlic powder
Salt and freshly ground black pepper, to taste
1 tbsp. unsalted butter, melted
For serving:
Blue cheese dressing
Celery
Carrot sticks

1. Place the chicken wings on a large plate, then sprinkle evenly with the baking powder, cayenne, and garlic powder. Toss the wings with your hands, making sure the baking powder and seasonings fully coat them, until evenly incorporated. Let the wings stand in the refrigerator for 1 hour or up to overnight.
2. Preheat the air fryer to 200ºC.
3. Season the wings with salt and black pepper, then transfer to the air fryer, standing them up on end against the air fryer basket wall and each other. Air fry for 20 minutes, or until the wings are cooked through and crisp and golden brown. Transfer the wings to a bowl and toss with the butter while they're hot.
4. Arrange the wings on a platter and serve warm with the blue cheese dressing, celery and carrot sticks.

Lemony Chicken Drumsticks

SERVES 2

| **PREP TIME:** 5 minutes
| **COOK TIME:** 30 minutes

2 tsps. freshly ground coarse black pepper
1 tsp. baking powder
½ tsp. garlic powder
4 chicken drumsticks (113 g each)
Salt, to taste
1 lemon

1. In a small bowl, stir together the pepper, baking powder, and garlic powder. Place the drumsticks on a plate and sprinkle evenly with the baking powder mixture, turning the drumsticks so they're well coated. Let the drumsticks stand in the refrigerator for at least 1 hour or up to overnight.
2. Preheat the air fryer to 190ºC.
3. Sprinkle the drumsticks with salt, then transfer them to the air fryer, standing them bone-end up and leaning against the wall of the air fryer basket. Air fry for 30 minutes, or until cooked through and crisp on the outside.
4. Transfer the drumsticks to a serving platter and finely grate the zest of the lemon over them while they're hot. Cut the lemon into wedges and serve with the warm drumsticks.

CHAPTER 8 | 51
Snacks and Desserts

Coconut-Crusted Prawns

SERVES 2-4

| **PREP TIME:** 10 minutes
| **COOK TIME:** 4 minutes

227 g medium prawns, peeled and deveined (tails intact)
240 ml canned coconut milk
Finely grated zest of 1 lime
salt, to taste
60 g panko bread crumbs
40 g unsweetened shredded coconut
Freshly ground black pepper, to taste
Cooking spray
1 small or ½ medium cucumber, halved and deseeded
245 g coconut yogurt
1 serrano chili, deseeded and minced

1. Preheat the air fryer to 200ºC.
2. In a bowl, combine the prawns, coconut milk, lime zest, and ½ tsp. salt. Let the prawns stand for 10 minutes.
3. Meanwhile, in a separate bowl, stir together the bread crumbs and shredded coconut and season with salt and pepper.
4. A few at a time, add the prawns to the bread crumb mixture and toss to coat completely. Transfer the prawns to a wire rack set over a baking sheet. Spray the prawns all over with cooking spray.
5. Transfer the prawns to the air fryer and air fry for 4 minutes, or until golden brown and cooked through. Transfer the prawns to a serving platter and season with more salt.
6. Grate the cucumber into a small bowl. Stir in the coconut yogurt and chili and season with salt and pepper. Serve alongside the prawns while they're warm.

BBQ Pork Ribs

SERVES 2

| **PREP TIME:** 5 minutes
| **COOK TIME:** 35 minutes

1 tbsp. salt
1 tbsp. dark brown sugar
1 tbsp. sweet paprika
1 tsp. garlic powder
1 tsp. onion powder
1 tsp. poultry seasoning
½ tsp. mustard powder
½ tsp. freshly ground black pepper
1 kg individually cut St. Louis–style pork spareribs

1. Preheat the air fryer to 180ºC.
2. In a large bowl, whisk together the salt, brown sugar, paprika, garlic powder, onion powder, poultry seasoning, mustard powder, and pepper. Add the ribs and toss. Rub the seasonings into them with your hands until they're fully coated.
3. Arrange the ribs in the air fryer basket, standing up on their ends and leaned up against the wall of the basket and each other. Roast for 35 minutes, or until the ribs are tender inside and golden brown and crisp on the outside. Transfer the ribs to plates and serve hot.

CHAPTER 8
Snacks and Desserts

Spiced Sweet Potato Fries

SERVES 2

| **PREP TIME:** 10 minutes
| **COOK TIME:** 15 minutes

2 tbsps. olive oil
1½ tsps. smoked paprika
1½ tsps. salt, plus more as needed
1 tsp. chili powder
½ tsp. ground cumin
½ tsp. ground turmeric
½ tsp. mustard powder
¼ tsp. cayenne pepper
2 medium sweet potatoes (about 284 g each), cut into wedges, 1-cm thick and 6-cm long
Freshly ground black pepper, to taste
147 g sour cream
1 garlic clove, grated

1. Preheat the air fryer to 200ºC.
2. In a large bowl, combine the olive oil, paprika, salt, chili powder, cumin, turmeric, mustard powder, and cayenne. Add the sweet potatoes, season with black pepper, and toss to evenly coat.
3. Transfer the sweet potatoes to the air fryer (save the bowl with the leftover oil and spices) and air fry for 15 minutes, shaking the basket halfway through, or until golden brown and crisp. Return the potato wedges to the reserved bowl and toss again while they are hot.
4. Meanwhile, in a small bowl, stir together the sour cream and garlic. Season with salt and black pepper and transfer to a serving dish.
5. Serve the potato wedges hot with the garlic sour cream.

Spiced Mixed Nuts

MAKES 2 CUPS

| **PREP TIME:** 5 minutes
| **COOK TIME:** 6 minutes

75 g raw cashews
75 g raw pecan halves
75 g raw walnut halves
75 g raw whole almonds
2 tbsps. olive oil
1 tbsp. light brown sugar
1 tsp. chopped fresh rosemary leaves
1 tsp. chopped fresh thyme leaves
1 tsp. salt
½ tsp. ground coriander
¼ tsp. onion powder
¼ tsp. freshly ground black pepper
⅛ tsp. garlic powder

1. Preheat the air fryer to 180ºC.
2. In a large bowl, combine all the ingredients and toss until the nuts are evenly coated in the herbs, spices, and sugar.
3. Scrape the nuts and seasonings into the air fryer and air fry for 6 minutes, or until golden brown and fragrant, shaking the basket halfway through.
4. Transfer the cocktail nuts to a bowl and serve warm.

Crispy Apple Chips

SERVES 1

| PREP TIME: 5 minutes
| COOK TIME: 25-35 minutes

1 Honeycrisp or Pink Lady apple

1. Preheat the air fryer to 150ºC.
2. Core the apple with an apple corer, leaving apple whole. Cut the apple into ¼-cm-thick slices.
3. Arrange the apple slices in the basket, staggering slices as much as possible. Air fry for 25 to 35 minutes, or until the chips are dry and some are lightly browned, turning 4 times with tongs to separate and rotate them from top to bottom.
4. Place the chips in a single layer on a wire rack to cool. Apples will become crisper as they cool. Serve immediately.

Simple Apple Turnovers

SERVES 4

| PREP TIME: 10 minutes
| COOK TIME: 10 minutes

1 apple, peeled, quartered, and thinly sliced
½ tsps. pumpkin pie spice
Juice of ½ lemon
1 tbsp. granulated sugar
Pinch of salt
6 sheets phyllo dough

1. Preheat the air fryer to 165ºC.
2. In a medium bowl, combine the apple, pumpkin pie spice, lemon juice, granulated sugar, and salt.
3. Cut the phyllo dough sheets into 4 equal pieces and place individual tbsps. of apple filling in the centre of each piece, then fold in both sides and roll from front to back.
4. Spray the air fryer basket with nonstick cooking spray, then place the turnovers in the basket and bake for 10 minutes or until golden brown.
5. Remove the turnovers from the air fryer and allow to cool on a wire rack for 10 minutes before serving.

54 | CHAPTER 8
Snacks and Desserts

Spice Cookies

SERVES 4

| PREP TIME: 15 minutes
| COOK TIME: 12 minutes

4 tbsps. unsalted butter, at room temperature
2 tbsps. agave nectar
1 large egg
2 tbsps. water
240 g almond flour
100 g sugar
2 tsps. ground ginger
1 tsp. ground cinnamon
½ tsp. freshly grated nutmeg
1 tsp. baking soda
¼ tsp. salt

1. Preheat the air fryer to 165ºC.
2. Line the bottom of the air fryer basket with parchment paper cut to fit.
3. In a large bowl using a hand mixer, beat together the butter, agave, egg, and water on medium speed until fluffy.
4. Add the almond flour, sugar, ginger, cinnamon, nutmeg, baking soda, and salt. Beat on low speed until well combined.
5. Roll the dough into 2-tbsp. balls and arrange them on the parchment paper in the basket. (They don't really spread too much, but try to leave a little room between them.) Bake for 12 minutes, or until the tops of cookies are lightly browned.
6. Transfer to a wire rack and let cool completely.
7. Serve immediately.

Pineapple Galette

SERVES 2

| PREP TIME: 10 minutes
| COOK TIME: 40 minutes

¼ medium-size pineapple, peeled, cored, and cut crosswise into ½-cm thick slices
2 tbsps. dark rum
1 tsp. vanilla extract
½ tsp. salt
Finely grated zest of ½ lime
1 store-bought sheet puff pastry, cut into an 16-cm round
3 tbsps. granulated sugar
2 tbsps. unsalted butter, cubed and chilled
Coconut ice cream, for serving

1. Preheat the air fryer to 155ºC.
2. In a small bowl, combine the pineapple slices, rum, vanilla, salt, and lime zest and let stand for at least 10 minutes to allow the pineapple to soak in the rum.
3. Meanwhile, press the puff pastry round into the bottom and up the sides of a round metal cake pan and use the tines of a fork to dock the bottom and sides.
4. Arrange the pineapple slices on the bottom of the pastry in more or less a single layer, then sprinkle with the sugar and dot with the butter. Drizzle with the leftover juices from the bowl. Put the pan in the air fryer and bake until the pastry is puffed and golden brown and the pineapple is lightly caramelized on top, about 40 minutes.
5. Transfer the pan to a wire rack to cool for 15 minutes. Unmold the galette from the pan and serve warm with coconut ice cream.

Rosemary-Garlic Shoestring Fries

SERVES 2

| PREP TIME: 5 minutes
| COOK TIME: 18 minutes

1 large russet potato (340 g), scrubbed clean, and julienned
1 tbsp. vegetable oil
Leaves from 1 sprig fresh rosemary
Salt and freshly ground black pepper, to taste
1 garlic clove, thinly sliced
Flaky sea salt, for serving

1. Preheat the air fryer to 200°C.
2. Place the julienned potatoes in a large colander and rinse under cold running water until the water runs clear. Spread the potatoes out on a double-thick layer of paper towels and pat dry.
3. In a large bowl, combine the potatoes, oil, and rosemary. Season with salt and pepper and toss to coat evenly. Place the potatoes in the air fryer and air fry for 18 minutes, shaking the basket every 5 minutes and adding the garlic in the last 5 minutes of cooking, or until the fries are golden brown and crisp.
4. Transfer the fries to a plate and sprinkle with flaky sea salt while they're hot. Serve immediately.

Crispy Spiced Chickpeas

MAKES 1½ CUPS

| PREP TIME: 5 minutes
| COOK TIME: 6-12 minutes

1 can (425-g) chickpeas, rinsed and dried with paper towels
1 tbsp. olive oil
½ tsp. dried rosemary
½ tsp. dried parsley
½ tsp. dried chives
¼ tsp. mustard powder
¼ tsp. sweet paprika
¼ tsp. cayenne pepper
Salt and freshly ground black pepper, to taste

1. Preheat the air fryer to 180°C.
2. In a large bowl, combine all the ingredients, except for the salt and black pepper, and toss until the chickpeas are evenly coated in the herbs and spices.
3. Scrape the chickpeas and seasonings into the air fryer and air fry for 6 to 12 minutes, or until browned and crisp, shaking the basket halfway through.
4. Transfer the crispy chickpeas to a bowl, sprinkle with salt and black pepper, and serve warm.

Bacon-Wrapped Prawns and Jalapeño

SERVES 8

| PREP TIME: 20 minutes
| COOK TIME: 26 minutes

24 large prawn, peeled and deveined, about 340 g
5 tbsps. barbecue sauce, divided
12 strips bacon, cut in half
24 small pickled jalapeño slices

1. Toss together the prawns and 3 tbsps. of the barbecue sauce. Let stand for 15 minutes. Soak 24 wooden toothpicks in water for 10 minutes. Wrap 1 piece bacon around the prawn and jalapeño slice, then secure with a toothpick.
2. Preheat the air fryer to 180°C.
3. Working in batches, place half of the prawns in the air fryer basket, spacing them 1-cm apart. Air fry for 10 minutes. Turn prawns over with tongs and air fry for 3 minutes more, or until bacon is golden brown and prawns are cooked through.
4. Brush with the remaining barbecue sauce and serve.

CHAPTER 8
Snacks and Desserts

Baked Ricotta

MAKES 2 CUPS

| PREP TIME: 10 minutes
| COOK TIME: 15 minutes

1 (425-g) container whole milk Ricotta cheese
3 tbsps. grated Parmesan cheese, divided
2 tbsps. extra-virgin olive oil
1 tsp. chopped fresh thyme leaves
1 tsp. grated lemon zest
1 clove garlic, crushed with press
¼ tsp. salt
¼ tsp. pepper
Toasted baguette slices or crackers, for serving

1. Preheat the air fryer to 190ºC.
2. To get the baking dish in and out of the air fryer, create a sling using a 48-cm length of foil, folded lengthwise into thirds.
3. Whisk together the Ricotta, 2 tbsps. of the Parmesan, oil, thyme, lemon zest, garlic, salt, and pepper. Pour into a baking dish. Cover the dish tightly with foil.
4. Place the sling under dish and lift by the ends into the air fryer, tucking the ends of the sling around the dish. Bake for 10 minutes. Remove the foil cover and sprinkle with the remaining 1 tbsp. of the Parmesan. Air fry for 5 more minutes, or until bubbly at edges and the top is browned.
5. Serve warm with toasted baguette slices or crackers.

Lemony Apple Butter

MAKES 1¼ CUPS

| PREP TIME: 10 minutes
| COOK TIME: 1 hour

Cooking spray
500 g unsweetened applesauce
113 g packed light brown sugar
3 tbsps. fresh lemon juice
½ tsp. salt
¼ tsp. ground cinnamon
⅛ tsp. ground allspice

1. Preheat the air fryer to 170ºC.
2. Spray a metal cake pan with cooking spray. Whisk together all the ingredients in a bowl until smooth, then pour into the greased pan. Set the pan in the air fryer and bake until the apple mixture is caramelized, reduced to a thick purée, and fragrant, about 1 hour.
3. Remove the pan from the air fryer, stir to combine the caramelized bits at the edge with the rest, then let cool completely to thicken.
4. Serve immediately.

CHAPTER 9
Fast and Easy Everyday Favourites

Air Fried Broccoli ················· 59

Cheesy Potato Burgers ·················· 59

Crispy Chickpeas ················ 60

Simple and Easy Croutons ·············· 60

Sweet Corn and Carrot Fritters ············ 61

Lemony Pear Chips ················· 61

Bistro Potato Wedges ················ 62

Carrot and Celery Croquettes ············· 62

Spinach and Carrot Balls ················ 63

Simple Pea Delight ················ 63

Air Fried Broccoli

SERVES 1

| PREP TIME: 5 minutes
| COOK TIME: 6 minutes

4 egg yolks
56 g butter, melted
250 g coconut flour
Salt and pepper, to taste
140 g broccoli florets

1. Preheat the air fryer to 200ºC.
2. In a bowl, whisk the egg yolks and melted butter together. Throw in the coconut flour, salt and pepper, then stir again to combine well.
3. Dip each broccoli floret into the mixture and place in the air fryer basket. Air fry for 6 minutes in batches if necessary. Take care when removing them from the air fryer and serve immediately.

Cheesy Potato Burgers

SERVES 8

| PREP TIME: 5 minutes
| COOK TIME: 10 minutes

907 g white potatoes
30 g finely chopped spring onions
½ tsp. freshly ground black pepper, or more to taste
1 tbsp. fine sea salt
½ tsp. hot paprika
200 g shredded Colby cheese
60 ml rapeseed oil
110 g crushed crackers

1. Preheat the air fryer to 180ºC.
2. Boil the potatoes until soft. Dry them off and peel them before mashing thoroughly, leaving no lumps.
3. Combine the mashed potatoes with spring onions, pepper, salt, paprika, and cheese.
4. Mold the mixture into balls with your hands and press with your palm to flatten them into patties.
5. In a shallow dish, combine the rapeseed oil and crushed crackers. Coat the patties in the crumb mixture.
6. Bake the patties for about 10 minutes, in multiple batches if necessary. Serve hot.

Crispy Chickpeas

SERVES 4

| **PREP TIME:** 5 minutes
| **COOK TIME:** 15 minutes

1 (425-g) can chickpeas, drained but not rinsed
2 tbsps. olive oil
1 tsp. salt
2 tbsps. lemon juice

1. Preheat the air fryer to 200ºC.
2. Add all the ingredients together in a bowl and mix. Transfer this mixture to the air fryer basket.
3. Air fry for 15 minutes, ensuring the chickpeas become nice and crispy.
4. Serve immediately.

Simple and Easy Croutons

SERVES 4

| **PREP TIME:** 5 minutes
| **COOK TIME:** 8 minutes

2 slices friendly bread
1 tbsp. olive oil
Hot soup, for serving

1. Preheat the air fryer to 200ºC.
2. Cut the slices of bread into medium-size chunks.
3. Brush the air fryer basket with the oil.
4. Place the chunks inside and air fry for at least 8 minutes.
5. Serve with hot soup.

Sweet Corn and Carrot Fritters

SERVES 4

| PREP TIME: 10 minutes
| COOK TIME: 8-11 minutes

1 medium-sized carrot, grated
1 yellow onion, finely chopped
113 g canned sweet corn kernels, drained
1 tsp. sea salt flakes
1 tbsp. chopped fresh coriander
1 medium-sized egg, whisked
2 tbsps. plain milk
90 g grated Parmesan cheese
30 g flour
⅓ tsp. baking powder
⅓ tsp. sugar
Cooking spray

1. Preheat the air fryer to 180ºC.
2. Place the grated carrot in a colander and press down to squeeze out any excess moisture. Dry it with a paper towel.
3. Combine the carrots with the remaining ingredients.
4. Mold 1 tbsp. of the mixture into a ball and press it down with your hand or a spoon to flatten it. Repeat until the rest of the mixture is used up.
5. Spritz the balls with cooking spray.
6. Arrange in the air fryer basket, taking care not to overlap any balls. Bake for 8 to 11 minutes, or until they're firm.
7. Serve warm.

Lemony Pear Chips

SERVES 4

| PREP TIME: 15 minutes
| COOK TIME: 9-13 minutes

2 firm Bosc pears, cut crosswise into ¼-cm-thick slices
1 tbsp. freshly squeezed lemon juice
½ tsp. ground cinnamon
⅛ tsp. ground cardamom

1. Preheat the air fryer to 190ºC.
2. Separate the smaller stem-end pear rounds from the larger rounds with seeds. Remove the core and seeds from the larger slices. Sprinkle all slices with lemon juice, cinnamon, and cardamom.
3. Put the smaller chips into the air fryer basket. Air fry for 3 to 5 minutes, or until light golden brown, shaking the basket once during cooking. Remove from the air fryer.
4. Repeat with the larger slices, air frying for 6 to 8 minutes, or until light golden brown, shaking the basket once during cooking.
5. Remove the chips from the air fryer. Cool and serve or store in an airtight container at room temperature up for to 2 days.

CHAPTER 8
Snacks and Desserts

Bistro Potato Wedges

SERVES 4

| PREP TIME: 10 minutes
| COOK TIME: 13 minutes

454 g fingerling potatoes, cut into wedges
1 tsp. extra-virgin olive oil
½ tsp. garlic powder
Salt and pepper, to taste
75 g raw cashews, soaked in water overnight
½ tsp. ground turmeric
½ tsp. paprika
1 tbsp. nutritional yeast
1 tsp. fresh lemon juice
30 ml to 60 ml water

1. Preheat the air fryer to 200ºC.
2. In a bowl, toss together the potato wedges, olive oil, garlic powder, and salt and pepper, making sure to coat the potatoes well.
3. Transfer the potatoes to the air fryer basket and air fry for 10 minutes.
4. In the meantime, prepare the cheese sauce. Pulse the cashews, turmeric, paprika, nutritional yeast, lemon juice, and water together in a food processor. Add more water to achieve your desired consistency.
5. When the potatoes are finished cooking, transfer to a bowl and add the cheese sauce on top. Air fry for an additional 3 minutes.
6. Serve hot.

Carrot and Celery Croquettes

SERVES 4

| PREP TIME: 10 minutes
| COOK TIME: 6 minutes

2 medium-sized carrots, trimmed and grated
2 medium-sized celery stalks, trimmed and grated
30 g finely chopped leek
1 tbsp. garlic paste
¼ tsp. freshly cracked black pepper
1 tsp. fine sea salt
1 tbsp. finely chopped fresh dill
1 egg, lightly whisked
30 g flour
¼ tsp. baking powder
60 g bread crumbs
Cooking spray
Chive mayo, for serving

1. Preheat the air fryer to 180ºC.
2. Drain any excess liquid from the carrots and celery by placing them on a paper towel.
3. Stir together the vegetables with all of the other ingredients, save for the bread crumbs and chive mayo.
4. Use your hands to mold 1 tbsp. of the vegetable mixture into a ball and repeat until all of the mixture has been used up. Press down on each ball with your hand or a palette knife. Cover completely with bread crumbs. Spritz the croquettes with cooking spray.
5. Arrange the croquettes in a single layer in the air fryer basket and air fry for 6 minutes.
6. Serve warm with the chive mayo on the side.

Spinach and Carrot Balls

SERVES 4

PREP TIME: 10 minutes **COOK TIME:** 10 minutes	2 slices toasted bread 1 carrot, peeled and grated 1 package fresh spinach, blanched and chopped ½ onion, chopped 1 egg, beaten ½ tsp. garlic powder 1 tsp. minced garlic 1 tsp. salt ½ tsp. black pepper 1 tbsp. nutritional yeast 1 tbsp. flour

1. Preheat the air fryer to 200ºC.
2. In a food processor, pulse the toasted bread to form bread crumbs. Transfer into a shallow dish or bowl.
3. In a bowl, mix together all the other ingredients.
4. Use your hands to shape the mixture into small-sized balls. Roll the balls in the bread crumbs, ensuring to cover them well.
5. Put in the air fryer basket and air fry for 10 minutes.
6. Serve immediately.

Simple Pea Delight

SERVES 2-4

PREP TIME: 5 minutes **COOK TIME:** 15 minutes	125 g flour 1 tsp. baking powder 3 eggs 240 ml coconut milk 225 g cream cheese 3 tbsps. pea protein 70 g chicken or turkey strips Pinch of sea salt 225 g Mozzarella cheese

1. Preheat the air fryer to 200ºC.
2. In a large bowl, mix all ingredients together using a large wooden spoon.
3. Spoon equal amounts of the mixture into muffin cups and bake for 15 minutes.
4. Serve immediately.

Appendix 1 Air Fryer Time Table

Vegetable					
Item	Temp(°C)	Time (mins)	Item	Temp(°C)	Time (mins)
Asparagus (sliced 2-cm)	205°C	5	Mushrooms (sliced ½-cm)	205°C	5
Aubergine (4-cm cubes)	205°C	15	Onions (pearl)	205°C	10
Beetroots (whole)	205°C	40	Parsnips (1-cm chunks)	195°C	15
Broccoli (florets)	205°C	6	Peppers (2-cm chunks)	205°C	15
Brussels Sprouts (halved)	195°C	15	Potatoes (small baby, 650 g)	205°C	14
Carrots (sliced 1-cm)	195°C	15	Potatoes (2-cm chunks)	205°C	12
Cauliflower (florets)	205°C	12	Potatoes (baked whole)	205°C	40
Corn on the cob	200°C	6	Runner Beans	205°C	5
Courgette (1-cm sticks)	205°C	12	Sweet Potato (baked)	195°C	30 to 35
Fennel (quartered)	190°C	15	Tomatoes (cherry)	205°C	4
Kale leaves	120°C	12	Tomatoes (halves)	180°C	10

Chicken

Item	Temp (°C)	Time (mins)	Item	Temp(°C)	Time (mins)
Breasts, bone in (550 g)	190°C	24	Legs, bone in (800 g)	195°C	30
Breasts, boneless (150 g)	195°C	14	Wings (900 g)	205°C	12
Drumsticks (1.1 kg)	190°C	20	Game Hen (halved – 900 g)	200°C	20
Thighs, bone in (900 g)	195°C	22	Whole Chicken (3 kg)	185°C	75
Thighs, boneless (700 g)	195°C	20	Tenders	185°C	8 to 10

Beef

Item	Temp (°C)	Time (mins)	Item	Temp(°C)	Time (mins)
Burger (120 g)	190°C	16 to 20	Meatballs (7-cm)	195°C	10
Filet Mignon (250 g)	205°C	18-20	Ribeye, bone in (2-cm, 250 g)	205°C	12 to 15
Flank Steak (700 g)	205°C	13	Sirloin steaks (2-cm, 350 g)	205°C	10 to 14
London Broil (900 g)	205°C	20 to 28	Beef Eye Round Roast (1.8 kg)	200°C	45 to 55
Meatballs (2-cm)	195°C	7			

APPENDIX

Pork and Lamb

Item	Temp (°C)	Time (mins)	Item	Temp(°C)	Time (mins)
Loin (900 g)	185°C	55	Bacon (thick cut)	205°C	6 to 10
Pork Chops, bone in (2-cm, 200 g)	205°C	13	Sausages	195°C	15
Tenderloin (450 g)	190°C	15	Lamb Loin Chops (2-cm thick)	205°C	8 to 12
Bacon (regular)	205°C	5 to 7	Rack of lamb (600-1000 g)	195°C	23

Fish and Seafood

Item	Temp (°C)	Time (mins)	Item	Temp(°C)	Time (mins)
Calamari (250 g)	205°C	5	Tuna steak	205°C	7 to 10
Fish Fillet (2-cm, 250 g)	205°C	12	Scallops	205°C	5 to 7
Salmon, fillet (200 g)	195°C	12-14	Prawn	205°C	5
Swordfish steak	205°C	10			

Frozen Foods					
Item	Temp (°C)	Time (mins)	Item	Temp(°C)	Time (mins)
Onion Rings (350 g)	205°C	9	Fish Fingers (300 g)	205°C	11
Thin Chips (550 g)	205°C	13	Fish Fillets (1-cm, 300 g)	205°C	15
Thick Chips (500 g)	205°C	20	Chicken Nuggets (350 g)	205°C	10
Mozzarella Sticks (300 g)	205°C	8	Breaded Prawn	205°C	9
Pot Stickers (300 g)	205°C	8			

APPENDIX 2: RECIPES INDEX

A

APPLE
Crispy Apple Chips	54
Simple Apple Turnovers	54

AUBERGINE
Ratatouille	13

AVOCADO
Gold Avocado	8

B

BACON
Egg and Bacon Muffins	7
Super Easy Bacon Cups	11
Bacon Eggs on the Go	9

BANANA
Banana Bread	10

BEEF
Provolone Stuffed Beef and Pork Meatballs	43
Smoked Beef	43
Classic Spring Rolls	43
Swedish Beef Meatballs	41
Lettuce Fajita Meatball Wraps	49

BEEF CUBE STEAK
Beef Steak Fingers	45

BEEF RIBEYE STEAK
Rosemary Ribeye Steaks	40

BEEF SCHNITZEL
Easy Beef Schnitzel	41

BROCCOLI
Air Fried Broccoli	59

C

CABBAGE
Super Veg Rolls	17

CARROT
Carrot and Celery Croquettes	62
Sweet Corn and Carrot Fritters	61

CASHEW
Spiced Mixed Nuts	53

CHICKEN
Simple Pea Delight	63

CHICKEN BREAST
Chicken Manchurian	28
Chicken with Pineapple and Peach	25
Roasted Chicken and Vegetable Salad	24
Cranberry Curry Chicken	20
Barbecue Chicken	22
Lemon Chicken and Spinach Salad	24
Buttermilk Paprika Chicken	27
Almond-Crusted Chicken Nuggets	20
Easy Tandoori Chicken	25
Air Fryer Chicken Fajitas	21
Lemon Garlic Chicken	28
Roasted Chicken with Garlic	27
Tex-Mex Chicken Breasts	26
Apricot-Glazed Chicken	23
Chicken Pita Sandwich	48

CHICKEN DRUMSTICK

Lemony Chicken Drumsticks	51
CHICKEN LEG	
Jerk Chicken Leg Quarters	21
CHICKEN THIGH	
Garlic Soy Chicken Thighs	23
Curried Orange Honey Chicken	26
CHICKEN WING	
Spicy Chicken Wings	51
CHICKPEA	
Crispy Chickpeas	60
Crispy Spiced Chickpeas	56
COD	
Crunchy Air Fried Cod Fillets	34
Roasted Cod with Lemon-Garlic Potatoes	37
CORN	
Nugget and Veggie Taco Wraps	47
COURGETTE	
Veggie Salsa Wraps	49
CRAB	
Crab Cakes with Lettuce and Apple Salad	32

F

FINGERLING POTATO	
Chili Fingerling Potatoes	15
Tandoori-Spiced Salmon and Potatoes	30
Bistro Potato Wedges	62

H

HADDOCK	
Air Fryer Fish Sticks	30
HALIBUT	
Moroccan Spiced Halibut with Chickpea Salad	35

P

PARSNIP	
Lush Vegetables Roast	18
PEAR	
Lemony Pear Chips	61
PINEAPPLE	
Pineapple Galette	55
PINK SALMON	
Simple Salmon Bites	36
PORK	
Hearty Sweet and Sour Pork	45
PORK BELLY	
Teriyaki Pork and Mushroom Rolls	42
PORK CHOP	
Vietnamese Pork Chops	42
PORK RIB	
Barbecue Pork Ribs	39
PORK SHOULDER	
Char Siew	40
PORK TENDERLOIN	
Simple Pulled Pork	39
POTATO	
Russet Potato Gratin	13
Ricotta Potatoes	16
Potato with Creamy Cheese	14
Roasted Potatoes and Asparagus	14
Rosemary-Garlic Shoestring Fries	56
PRAWN	
Thai Prawn Skewers with Peanut Dipping Sauce	34
Cheesy Prawn Sandwich	48

APPENDIX | 69

Coconut-Crusted Prawns	52
Bacon-Wrapped Prawns and Jalapeño	56

R

RED POTATO

Potato and Broccoli with Tofu Scramble	18

S

SALMON

Confetti Salmon Burgers	33
Roasted Salmon Fillets	31
Orange-Mustard Glazed Salmon	32

SAUSAGE

Parmesan Sausage Egg Muffins	10
Breakfast Sausage and Cauliflower	7

SEA SCALLOP

Bacon-Wrapped Scallops	33

SKIRT STEAK

Ritzy Skirt Steak Fajitas	44

SOLE

Sole and Asparagus Bundles	31

SPINACH

Spinach and Carrot Balls	63

ST. LOUIS–STYLE PORK SPARERIBS

BBQ Pork Ribs	52

SWEET POTATO

Sweet Potatoes with Courgette	17
Spiced Sweet Potato Fries	53

SWORDFISH

Swordfish Skewers with Caponata	36

T

TILAPIA

Pecan-Crusted Tilapia	35

TOFU

Tofu Bites	16
Sesame Taj Tofu	15

TOP ROUND STEAK

Beef and Vegetable Cubes	44

TUNA

Tuna and Lettuce Wraps	47
Tuna Muffin Sandwich	49

W

WALNUT

Posh Orange Rolls	11

WAX BEAN

Cracker Wax Beans	18

WHITE FISH

Vegetable and Fish Tacos	37

WHITE POTATO

Cheesy Potato Burgers	59

WHOLE CHICKEN

Whole Chicken Roast	22

Printed in Great Britain
by Amazon